info@kinfolk.com
www.kinfolk.com

Kinfolk Magazine
328 NE Failing Street
Portland, Oregon 97212
Telephone: 503-946-8400

Printed in Canada

Publication Design by Amanda Jane Jones
Cover Photograph by Neil Bedford

MADE & CRAFTED™
LEVI'S®

TOAST

WOMEN

MEN

HOUSE&HOME

WWW.TOA.ST

KINFOLK

NATHAN WILLIAMS
EDITOR IN CHIEF & CREATIVE DIRECTOR

GEORGIA FRANCES KING
EDITOR

GAIL O'HARA
MANAGING EDITOR

ANJA VERDUGO
ART DIRECTOR

AMANDA JANE JONES
LEAD DESIGNER

JENNIFER JAMES WRIGHT
DESIGN DIRECTOR

DOUG BISCHOFF
BUSINESS OPERATIONS

KATIE SEARLE-WILLIAMS
BUSINESS MANAGER

PAIGE BISCHOFF
ACCOUNTS PAYABLE & RECEIVABLE

JULIE POINTER
COMMUNITY DIRECTOR

JESSICA GRAY
COMMUNITY MANAGER

NATHAN TICKNOR
SERVICE MANAGER

JOANNA HAN
CONTRIBUTING EDITOR

KELSEY VALA
RECIPE EDITOR

KELSEY SNELL
PROOFREADER

ERIC DAVIS
WEB ADMINISTRATOR

ALYSSA HERZINGER
EDITORIAL & OPERATIONS ASSISTANT

SARAH ROWLAND
EDITORIAL ASSISTANT

MICHELLE CHO
COMMUNITY & DESIGN ASSISTANT

STEPHANIE GROSSE
BUSINESS ASSISTANT

EMMA LAUKITIS
OPERATIONS ASSISTANT

SUBSCRIBE

Kinfolk is published four times a year.
To subscribe, visit *www.kinfolk.com/shop*
or email us at *subscribe@kinfolk.com*

CONTACT US

If you have questions or comments, write to us at *info@kinfolk.com*
For advertising inquiries, get in touch at *advertise@kinfolk.com*

WWW.KINFOLK.COM

WELCOME

"There is a crack in everything—that's how the light gets in"

—LEONARD COHEN

Over the first three years of *Kinfolk*'s life, there have been ups and downs, lefts and rights, tosses and turns. Although most of these mishaps never make it into the pages of the magazine you now hold in your hands, the path we've trodden has occasionally veered off course and sent us tumbling into a pile of blackberry brambles (both proverbially and literally). Believe us—we are far from perfect. So we thought it was time to drop the veil and reveal unlucky number 13: The Imperfect Issue.

For our autumn edition, we'd like to celebrate the holes in our socks, our scorched attempts at marmalade-making and all the crappy haircuts we've had over the years. We're all guilty of occasionally attempting to make our lives seem a little cleaner or a bit more organized, but the reality is often quite different. Daydreaming of an idyllic life serves the valuable purpose of hopeful aspiration, but what if we dropped the facade for a moment and wholeheartedly accepted our shortcomings?

Within this issue, other cultures offer us lessons on embracing life's supposed flaws: Some generations of Navajo weavers create purposeful mistakes in their designs to free their minds from unattainable precision, and the Japanese art of *kintsugi* repair uses gold leaf to highlight the fractures in damaged ceramics. A Westminster Dog Show judge, an Olympic gymnastics evaluator and a Pulitzer Prize–winning restaurant critic weigh in on their attempts to empirically judge perfection, and a fine art conservator explains how some historical blemishes can actually add to a painting's story.

It turns out many things that appear to be faultless may not be: We uncover the differences between genetically identical twins, suggest ways to ease up on your overly uncluttered interior decorating style and interview Wendy Whelan— the 47-year-old principal ballerina for the New York City Ballet—about the pressure to be the very embodiment of aesthetic perfection (and making it look like a plié in the park).

The kitchen is also filled with some of the tastiest disasters around: You only need 10 minutes behind the scenes at a commercial kitchen or to watch a few episodes of Julia Child's *The French Chef* to know that no cook is perfect, including ourselves. We have some citrusy suggestions for what to make when life gives you lemons, a recipe for preemptively fallen cheese soufflé, an entire menu based around setting your food on fire and many more culinary mishaps.

From the shoddy darning on your cardigan to the oddly manicured shrubs in your neighborhood, these flawed details are the beautifully blemished collateral of a life lived to the fullest. So make mistakes. Make a mess. What have you got to lose?

NATHAN WILLIAMS AND GEORGIA FRANCES KING

NEIL BEDFORD
Photographer
London, United Kingdom

NILS BERNSTEIN
Writer
New York, New York

JENN BONNETT
Stylist
San Mateo, California

ALISON BRISLIN
Stylist
Portland, Oregon

RACHEL CAULFIELD
Stylist
London, United Kingdom

LIZ CLAYTON
Writer
Brooklyn, New York

KATRIN COETZER
Illustrator
Cape Town, South Africa

DAVID COGGINS
Writer
New York, New York

LAUREN COLTON
Stylist
Seattle, Washington

TRAVIS ELBOROUGH
Writer
London, United Kingdom

MARGARET EVERTON
Writer
Portland, Oregon

KARYN FIEBICH
Stylist
Portland, Oregon

PARKER FITZGERALD
Photographer
Portland, Oregon

MAIA FLORE
Photographer
Paris, France

SUZANNE FUOCO
Writer
Portland, Oregon

ALICE GAO
Photographer
New York, New York

JIM GOLDEN
Photographer
Portland, Oregon

HIDEAKI HAMADA
Photographer
Osaka, Japan

CHARLOTTE HEAL
Art Director
London, United Kingdom

TAE INO
Writer
Tokyo, Japan

SARAH JACOBY
Illustrator
Philadelphia, Pennsylvania

CRAIG JOHNSON
Photographer
Granite Bay, California

KATE S. JORDAN
Prop Stylist
Pound Ridge, New York

STEPHANIE ROSENBAUM KLASSEN
Writer
Sonoma, California

KATHRIN KOSCHITZKI
Photographer
Nuremberg, Germany

JOSS MCKINLEY
Photographer
New York, New York

NICOLÒ MINERBI
Photographer
San Francisco, California

BERTIL NILSSON
Photographer
London, United Kingdom

SAYURI SAKAIRI
Stylist
Berlin, Germany

CHARLIE SCHUCK
Photographer
Seattle, Washington

KENDRA SMOOT
Stylist
New York, New York

SETH SMOOT
Photographer
New York, New York

JOHN STANLEY
Writer
London, United Kingdom

SHANTANU STARICK
Photographer
Brisbane, Australia

KATIE STRATTON
Painter
Dayton, Ohio

KELSEY VALA
Writer
Portland, Oregon

NICOLE VARVITSIOTES
Writer
San Luis Obispo, California

HELLE WALSTED
Stylist & Producer
Copenhagen, Denmark

WE ARE THE RHOADS
Photographers
Los Angeles, California

WICHMANN + BENDTSEN
Photographers
Copenhagen, Denmark

MARTIN WUNDERWALD
Photographer
Dresden, Germany

DIANA YEN
Writer & Stylist
New York, New York

ONE

TWO

FEW

ONE

ENTERTAINING FOR ONE

○

GOING AGAINST THE GRAIN

WORDS BY STEPHANIE ROSENBAUM KLASSEN & PHOTOGRAPHS BY HIDEAKI HAMADA
STYLING BY SAYURI SAKAIRI

Ever felt like something just doesn't belong? The world can occasionally make us feel out of place in our own lives, but sometimes being the odd one out brings more joy than you may think.

When I told my mother I was leaving my pretty Brooklyn apartment to go live in a tent as a farming apprentice in Santa Cruz, I can't say she was surprised. I was her black sheep daughter after all: the feisty, opinionated youngest of three girls, the adventurer, the wanderer, the one with good stories instead of a mortgage, books instead of babies. Her address book was full of my constantly changing whereabouts—San Francisco, Italy, New York—scratched out in ink, scribbled in pencil, then finally jotted on Post-it notes stuck between the pages.

The East Coast suburbanites I grew up with would rather go to their beloved ballet naked than forgo a firm mattress and a decent thread count. So my willingness to do so for a six-month stretch must have provided much mirth to the whole extended clan. In their defense, this was seven years ago when "farm to table" hadn't caught on yet, and only a handful of people outside of Bolivia knew how to correctly pronounce *quinoa*, much less eat it for breakfast.

Then again, this kind of disruption and amusement is what families depend on their resident black sheep to provide. And why not? This unpredictable life, while sometimes precarious, is never boring. Hurtling down the road that others pass up, living out the vicarious fantasies of the stay-at-homes, we find joy in the sheer velocity, in the novelty of the unknown, sending back our stories scrawled on postcards, in letters with exotic stamps and emails tapped out over connections that flicker in and out as monsoon rains pound down.

"Do what you love!" they told me, and so I did, because I quickly discovered that I was next to useless at doing anything else. When I first became a restaurant critic, I could boast of nothing but a byline and the most minimal of paychecks. Only the blessing of a tiny rent-controlled apartment allowed me to live and work, yet investment bankers and corporate headhunters sat next to me at dinner parties and told me how much they wished for my job. "The crème brûlée reviewer… that's what I'd like to be," said one woman dreamily, her spoon forgotten halfway to her mouth. To them, my job was all sugary delight, far removed from their spreadsheets and mortgage payments, tedious meetings and office politics. And why ruin their fantasy? My currency was resourcefulness rather than cash. When one job ended, word passed through the grapevine about another. Rents were shared, clothes were secondhand, and as long as someone was having a gallery opening, wine was free. We looked out for each other, because outside of our outsiders' tribe, who else would watch over us?

A black sheep toughens up. Survival means learning to love what others deride. We may seem game and self-confident, but it's a resiliency won from rejection, from being the weirdos always picked last for kickball, the ones who talked too loudly, quoted Charles Bukowski, read Dorothy Allison, clowned for the spotlight or shriveled up when called on in class. Looking back now, we can see how those who took the safe path often envy us, the risk-takers. So let's raise a toast to creativity and quirks, to weirdness and bliss, to all the sheep of so many colors for carving out corners of beautiful oddity. ○

Stephanie Rosenbaum Klassen's most recent book is The Art of Vintage Cocktails. *After 20 years of living in San Francisco, she now lives in Sonoma, California, with her winemaker husband and their cat, Bubba.*

NATURAL JUDGMENT

*We don't scrutinize nature and remark on its flaws, so why not extend
that sense of wonder and awe to our fellow humans? Paired with a
collection of San Francisco's oddly shaped shrubs, this essay encourages
us to accept the blemishes in the world around us.*

WORDS BY JULIE POINTER & PHOTOGRAPHS BY NICOLÒ MINERBI

Something remarkable happens when we step into the natural world: We put down our judge's gavel and take up the observer's binoculars instead. The critical eye softens and opens anew upon whatever weird, fascinating or beautiful detail the world may have to offer. We're no less impressed by the stately oak because of its galls or by the gray whale because of her unsightly belly barnacles—it hardly occurs to us that these marks should be considered flaws. At the Grand Canyon or in the presence of a bald eagle, we don't remark on how these wonders could be improved upon, but rather marvel that these creations manage to be so uniquely and recklessly themselves.

Comparison steals our joy. We dwell in urban places where self-consciousness reigns and assessment runs high. The only place we're completely removed from under (or behind) the microscope is when we immerse ourselves in nature and leave the mirror of society behind. I can't recall when I've looked at a sycamore in autumn and wondered why the leaves weren't more orange, or why the foliage wasn't just a bit slimmer. Lumpy clouds are just as welcome as wispy ones, and though I curse the raccoon as he's rummaging through my trash, I don't question why his eyes are so close together or begrudge him for his slender wrists.

There's no accepted judgment system for nature in the kind of formal, subjective way that we think about people in our daily lives. We make measurements about our fellow humans willy-nilly as we go about our days, based wholly on external factors. In contrast, we hardly think about the possibility of imperfection within a towering stand of redwoods or at the edge of the expansive Atlantic. The intricacies found in the natural world provoke a feeling of respect that the earth manages to carry on in the face of her so-called blemishes.

If I fix my mind on the elm tree outside my window and consider that it may produce as many as six million leaves each season, I'm bewildered with the kind of curiosity I wish I could cast upon the people I encounter. What if I shifted this focused amazement for Mother Earth onto the human beings around me? What kind of radical would I become if I started imagining the astonishing number of arteries, capillaries, ventricles and vesicles within the man sitting next to me on the airplane, instead of how irritating his loud breathing and elbow-grinding has become? Would my eyes not start seeing sublime curiosities at every turn?

And here's where a healthy dose of awe can step in as the great equalizer. Our unbiased appreciation of nature prods us beyond our shallow framework for calculating worth and forces us to see with clearer eyes. The notion of striving for superficial human perfection fades when we consider the mystery of every human being. If we could manage to recover our sense of curiosity, we might find ourselves vying to be only and completely ourselves, and in turn, expecting and emboldening the same within others. ○

Julie Pointer is the community director at Kinfolk. *She is a maker, writer and art director living in Portland, Oregon, dreaming of one day running her own inn and artist retreat.*

WEAR AND TEAR

WORDS BY DAVID COGGINS

PHOTOGRAPHS BY SETH SMOOT & STYLING BY KENDRA SMOOT

When it comes to clothing, relationships and most other things in life, chasing perfection is pointless. It's how you flaunt your flaws that matters.

Is it possible that white shoes can provide insight into the world? Over the years I've cultivated an appreciation for white bucks, spectators, cricket shoes and more bucks (which I fully support wearing from early spring deep into Indian summer). When you acquire white shoes, they embody perfection, unsullied by the world, without a trace of age. There's nothing wrong with admiring your new pair for days—even weeks—before wearing them. I've even got an unworn pair that's been waiting gracefully in my closet for a few years.

But in this Platonic state, they don't yet exist the way the sartorial gods intended. They're not yet worn, they're not yet tarnished, they're not yet truly *yours*. White shoes don't remain white, nor should they. They should reflect that trip to New Orleans, the time you were caught in the rain or the grass stain from a lawn bowling escapade. Conversely, it's only then that they achieve white shoe nirvana.

We're attracted to things that show a sense of their history and are honest: the boxer's broken nose, flawed heroes, the singer's aging voice. Fred Astaire threw his suits against the wall (or had his valet do it) to take the newness out of them. He knew that a suit shouldn't look fresh; it should look lived in and reflect its wearer, not its maker. After all, he was born Frederick Austerlitz, so he knew the power of reinvention better than anyone.

I confirmed this theory a few years ago when I ran into a particularly well-dressed friend on one of the hottest days of summer. He was wearing a gray suit, a yellow tie and white shoes, and he looked immaculate. When I got closer, I realized he had a dark footprint across the top of one buck. It was brilliant. The stain, in the context of everything else, was inspired. He knew that flaws were an inherent part of life, and he embraced that.

You overlook the seeming mistakes of a well-dressed man: He doesn't mind that his collar is frayed, so you don't either. These people teach us that there are more important things than perfection. For example, I remember this old red leather couch in the Jack Spade store on Greene Street in Manhattan. Every time it ripped, they just put more duct tape on it and pretty soon it was more tape than couch. Whenever I walked into the store, I was happy to see it was still there. I developed an attachment to it that I never would've had to an immaculate club chair.

All of which is to say, there's a danger that the quest for perfectionism becomes an end unto itself. There's more to the world than acquisition: The best interiors can't just be bought any more than style can. As I get older, that's one reason I find myself attracted to those whose style is eccentric rather than immaculate. But that can't be achieved in a day. A pair of faux-distressed jeans isn't going to do the trick, so you're going to have to break them in yourself. Yes, you can track down something worn-in on eBay, but that's not the same thing, and secretly we all know it. In the end, we all have to make our own way down the long, rewarding path toward hard-earned individuality, with all of its flaws. ○

David Coggins has come to terms with his eccentric side. His writing has appeared in Esquire, Interview *and* Art in America, *among other places. He lives in New York.*

JULIA CHILD'S GUIDE TO COOKING TERRIBLY

WORDS BY NILS BERNSTEIN & PHOTOGRAPH BY ANJA VERDUGO

"Try new recipes, learn from your mistakes, be fearless and above all have fun." These words started a culinary coup in the kitchen where, for the first time, we were encouraged to make a mess as well as dinner.

The American cooking revolution came in the form of a six-foot-two college basketball player, WWII vet and cookbook author named Julia Child. With a plate of *boeuf bourguignon* on her 1960s television show *The French Chef*, she brought fine cuisine into our homes in the age of TV dinners. Stripping away the pretense of fancy dining with her breezy style, she always had a one-liner ready in her trademark singsong voice: "I enjoy cooking with wine—sometimes I even put it in the food!"

More importantly, Julia wasn't afraid to screw up like the best of us do, and she certainly wasn't afraid to do it on live TV. Unlike the picture-perfect, competitive nature of today's food television, which can intimidate more than encourage, she pushed millions to experiment with coq au vin and Grand Marnier soufflé, promising that we'd have dinner on the table instead of a delivery pizza, no matter what.

Julia celebrated the imperfections of home cooking and didn't believe in so-called failures: If you muck something up, then you should change tack or cover it with a tasty sauce. She once noted that "one of the secrets—and pleasures—of cooking is to learn to correct something if it goes awry, and one of the lessons is to grin and bear it if it cannot be fixed." The latter point allows for the serendipity that marks great home cooking—the delicious density of a fallen soufflé, lasagna with a crispy mottling of blackened cheese or the range of flavor in a leg of lamb that's part rare and part well-done. Maybe you actually prefer under-baked cookies, burned toast smothered in butter or swollen overcooked pasta—al dente be damned!

After all, we admire the random lumps of an heirloom tomato and rustic burgers that poke their way out of the bun. Processed and fast food companies have begun engineering their foodstuffs to mimic "homey" imperfections: Kraft turkey slices molded as uneven slabs, meandering McDonald's egg whites, craggy-edged "artisan" pizzas from Domino's. So why obsess over a piecrust crimp when you can shove the crust into a fruit filling and call it a pandowdy? Pasta cut or broken into random ribbons even has a fancy name: *maltagliati*.

On *The French Chef*, Julia once flubbed a potato pancake flip, quickly transferred it to a baking dish and then added cheese and cream, turning it into an invented recipe that was no doubt replicated in kitchens around the country. "You should never apologize at the table... in cooking you've got to have a what-the-hell attitude," she said—and she always practiced what she preached. For another example, look up her famous 1987 *Letterman* appearance when a burner failed and she transformed raw hamburger meat and some cheese into a blowtorched *beef tartare gratiné* instead ("It's very chic, David," she insisted).

Julia's kitchen wisdom can also be applied to life. Ultimately, at the same time she was imploring us to have fun with our foibles and not beat ourselves up, she was a psychologist as much as our cooking teacher. "Maybe the cat has fallen into the stew or the lettuce has frozen or the cake has collapsed—*eh bien, tant pis!*" she said. "Usually one's cooking is better than one thinks it is." ○

Nils Bernstein works by day as a music publicist. His writing has appeared in Bon Appétit, Men's Journal *and* Wine Enthusiast. *He lives in New York but escapes to Mexico City every chance he gets.*

Read our Julia Child–inspired recipe for Fallen Cheese Soufflé on page 143.

GETTING SNIPPY

WORDS BY GAIL O'HARA & PHOTOGRAPH BY PARKER FITZGERALD

A hair stylist can change your life—for better or worse.
From childhood bowl cuts to traumatizing over-cuts, sometimes
it can be better to take your hairdo into your own hands.

Sometimes we end up in a hair stylist's chair when what we really need is a therapist's chaise. Gazing into a salon mirror can be way more revealing than we want it to be: What are you *really* doing there? Are your expectations for the scissor-wielder perhaps a bit too high? Do you imagine you can look just like Amélie when your mop is actually more Pippi Longstocking? Whether you've dreamed of having cornrows, a long bob or a Joan Jett, chances are you've felt that joy-pain-shock-horror of unmet expectations that come from yearning for a change that goes beyond your bangs.

A good haircut can change your life, and a bad one can have devastating effects. We've all been there, staring in disbelief as the person hacking away turns your perfectly passable head of hair into a mangled mohawk or an ill-advised pompadour. You brought in a photo of Carey Mulligan but left looking like Hillary Clinton. I once had my shoulder-length mane mulletized on the sides *without my consent* by a drag queen who wanted to "create the illusion that my hair was pulled back." Other snippers have given me layers that left me sporting a mushroom-cloud shag with wispy bits underneath. And while having great hair is great, having perfect hair is unnecessary. Consider the punk/new wave heyday of the late '70s and early '80s: Reacting to the floppy hippie hair of the preceding era, the kids grabbed the bleach, buzzers and Manic Panic, and did it themselves.

Stylists have the power to transform the shape of your head and the delicate state of your self-esteem. But sometimes what we expect from them—perfect hair or a life makeover—is a goal we can't attain. As the saying goes: "They're beauticians, not magicians." Ask any girl who has had the guts to chop off her own long, lustrous locks and go super-short: Having a self-inflicted haircut (or one given to you by your amateur friends) can be freeing and liberating.

A GUIDE TO CUTTING YOUR OWN HAIR

CHOP CHOP Use a wide-tooth comb and small, sharp scissors (ideally made for cutting hair) and remember to hold them vertically, not horizontally. Protect your eyes and have a friend there to spot you. Go very slowly. Experts advise not attempting this after multiple margaritas.

DON'T FIGHT NATURE When styling, work with what you have. If that means big fluffy hair, don't use a blow-dryer as it'll only make it even bigger. If you have curly hair, don't have it chemically straightened: Use some non-gelatinous hair product instead to give your gentle waves a nice teen-idol vibe. If you're born raven-haired, you may have difficulty achieving a platinum blonde hue (if you don't want it to fall out, that is).

PERSONAL STYLE Maintaining the shape of short hair can be lots of work. If you can afford regular trims, then go with a crazy asymmetrical do. If not, get an easier style to control. These days it's hard to get a decent haircut for less than $75, so we all need to be crafty. The painful reality is this: The haircut you get from a professional can be just as bad—or worse—than one you do on your own. If it's all a crapshoot anyway, then why not get snipping yourself? ○

Gail O'Hara has been shearing her own bangs regularly since the mid-2000s, with a success rate of about 80 percent. She is the managing editor of Kinfolk *and the publisher of* chickfactor.

TASTE OF FATE

Whether through spite, misfortune or pure laziness, some of the world's greatest culinary delights were actually invented by accident.

WORDS BY ALYSSA HERZINGER &
ILLUSTRATIONS BY KATRIN COETZER

THE SANDWICH Necessity certainly mothered invention when, while engrossed in a game of cards, the Earl of Sandwich demanded his meat be brought to him between two slices of bread so he could keep his hands clean and ready to lay down a royal flush. While it's doubtful he was the first to think up this simple combination, at least the Earl gave it a more exciting name than "meat in bread."

ICE CREAM CONES Although the first edible ice cream cone can be traced back to Europe in the 1800s, its debut as we know it now was in St. Louis, Missouri. One sweltering day during the 1904 World's Fair, an ice cream vendor ran out of serving dishes but saw salvation in a neighboring vendor's thin, waffle-like pastries. Joining forces, they served ice cream in these rolled-up vessels, giving the world an even higher calorie summer treat for years to come.

POTATO CHIPS This sodium-dusted lore trails back to 1853 at a resort in Saratoga Springs, New York. After a diner supposedly sent back plate after plate of french fries, complaining they were too thick and needed more salt, the spiteful cook served the customer paper-thin slices of potato, fried to a crisp and drowned in salt. Despite the cook's intentions, the customer loved them and nobody's been able to eat just one ever since.

TARTE TATIN According to legend, one of the two sisters who ran the Hotel Tatin in France was busy in the kitchen and nearly burned some apples she was cooking for a dessert. Thinking quickly, she covered the apples with a layer of pastry, baked it for a while to brown the dough and flipped it upside down to discover the apples perfectly caramelized. The dish became the sisters' specialty during the late 1800s, and their hometown of Lamotte-Beuvron is still known for it today.

CORN FLAKES In 1894, while experimenting with whole grain foods in a Victorian attempt to curb improper appetites, John Harvey Kellogg accidentally left some boiled wheat sitting out for too long. When he rolled it out, the wheat berries flattened into wide flakes that crisped when baked. His brother applied the same process to corn, and Kellogg's Corn Flakes quickly became a nationwide hit.

CHAMPAGNE In 17th-century France, a monk named Dom Pérignon faced a problem—the warming spring weather caused his bottled wines to undergo a second fermentation, which filled the wine with bubbles and burst open the bottles. Instead of trying to eliminate the pesky bubbles like other sommeliers, Dom Pérignon tested different grapes, processes and vessels, eventually creating his famous champagne.

CHEESE PUFFS According to one account from the 1930s, a livestock feed factory in Wisconsin used to pour wet cornmeal through their machines to prevent clogging. The cornmeal came out of the hot machine in puffy curls that were usually thrown away, until one day when an employee took some puffs home, added oil and cheese and brought them back to work. The cheesy puffs were such a hit in the factory that they began mass-producing them under the name Korn Kurls.

BEER One rainy day after humankind had discovered baking, the story goes that a bowl of fresh bread was mistakenly left outside. The forgotten loaves sat in the rainwater for a few days, and when the bakers finally remembered them, they found the bread submersed in a foamy golden liquid that was fermented by wild yeast. Not discriminating drinkers, they took a few sips and immediately realized what weekends had been missing.

SOURDOUGH Like beer, the first loaf of sourdough rose from a neglected heap of wild yeast. A few centuries ago, another forgetful cook mixed together some flour and water and let it sit for a few days, during which time the yeast in the air gobbled up the sugars in the flour. Upon returning to it, the cook found a bubbly batter, and through either laziness or genius, used it to leaven the next batch of bread, inadvertently baking the first tangy sourdough.

NACHOS In 1943, Ignacio "Nacho" Anaya scoured the kitchen for something to serve his lunch regulars when they requested a new appetizer. Starting with some freshly fried tortillas, he cut them into quarters and tossed on some grated cheese. Just before putting the plate into the oven, he added jalapeño slices. The customers devoured his creation, and the next day everyone was requesting Nacho's Special. ○

Alyssa Herzinger is a writer and actor based between the Pacific Northwest and Honolulu, Hawaii. She is currently pursuing an MA in French.

PHOTO ESSAY

THE WRONG SIDE OF THE BED

Some days you wake up late to a dead alarm clock, drop your cell phone in your coffee, leave the house with your skirt tucked into your tights and then step in a giant puddle all before 8 a.m. Here's to making peace with a day gone wrong.

PHOTOGRAPHS BY MAIA FLORE

3:00 A.M. It's one of those nights of absolute sleeplessness: Your mind races with meaningless trivia about everything except the best sheep-counting methods.

8:00 A.M. After finally submitting to a state of slumber, you oversleep and have to speed through your morning routine, leaving no time for making a cup of ever-important extra-strength home brew.

9:10 A.M. You somehow arrive at work on time(ish) and realize you forgot to look in a mirror earlier. You look like Cruella de Vil, but hopefully your coworkers think you're going through a rockabilly phase.

10:00 A.M. When you successfully slip out unnoticed to grab a latte, your clandestine attempts at caffeinating are thwarted when you pour most of it down your only clean shirt.

11:30 A.M. The internet is acting super slo-mo, which means you can't make a dent in your to-do list or procrastinate by looking at blogs "for research" on your phone.

1:30 P.M. After a tasteless lunch break, you realize you're not prepared for the afternoon meetings and your manager springs a last-minute deadline on you (as always).

4:45 P.M. You churn through your workload before dropping your slice of a workmate's birthday cake on the carpet. You go back for another to discover Craig from the third floor has finished the whole thing.

5:00 P.M. Walking out to your car, you notice that the birds have used it as a toilet. And your keys are locked inside, sitting on the front seat.

5:30 P.M. You end up taking the bus home instead, wondering if Mercury has gone retrograde or if the moon is full. Turns out it's both.

6:15 P.M. Search for the Thai takeout menu in the kitchen drawer. It's best to lighten up and laugh as you fall. In a world where everything happens way too fast, slow down, breathe, and pour yourself a scotch. ○

TO THE BITTER END

WORDS BY LIZ CLAYTON & PHOTOGRAPHS BY KATHRIN KOSCHITZKI

Marmalade-making is a maddening pursuit, often ending in gluggy goop, burned kitchen pots and citrus juice stinging sliced thumbs. To some, it's not worth the fight. For others, losing the battle is half the fun.

They say that baking is chemistry while cooking is art. If that's true, then making marmalade is like playing a game of chess on a constantly shifting board, where your pieces move in unpredictable directions and when your main opponent is yourself. (It's also very sticky.) This past miserable winter, I drowned my slim-pickins-for-fresh-produce blues in citrus, over and over and over, seeking bright orange distraction from the endless snow.

People are picky about marmalade: Countless parlor arguments debate flavor, sweetness, amount of peel or whether marmalade is even edible at all. Creating my own would give me control over finding that bitter, rindy balance I like best. And though I'm not a genius in the kitchen, I can follow a recipe. But as it turns out, that isn't enough.

Few things are more frustrating than making marmalade. You can use the same recipe, fruit and cookware, and one batch will set perfectly while the next hardens like glue and the last dribbles from your chilled saucer into infinity. My first attempt, which I viewed as an educational failure, seemed easy: It overset so quickly that I figured this jelling thing was no problem, I just had to back off a little. My second attempt? Perfect—just the right consistency and sweetness. But attempts three to eight were cruel jokes of fate, each failing differently than the batch before, finding me in an obsessive, dragon-chasing quest to repeat the ease of earlier congealments.

My disasters ranged between complete failure and emergency, each requiring some measure of re-canning, last-minute apple-juicing, re-boiling or simply throwing the batch in the garbage altogether. In humility and despair, I emailed a pastry chef friend who I'd secretly hoped to impress with my newfound prowess at something she was good at. "What's the secret? What am I doing wrong here?" I asked. "Every batch is different," she wrote back, unhelpfully adding that she usually worked "by eye."

Figuring out how to get it right became an addiction, and I somehow made it even harder. I noticed myself starting batches at the worst possible times: I'd soak fruit overnight when I'd only have an hour or two to prepare it the next day, or wander off to dissect eight overpriced, late-season Seville oranges right in the middle of a writing deadline. The scorched-sugar stains on my stove, cost of ingredients, time spent stirring and burned hands were bad enough, but the demoralization of not conquering this beast was much worse.

As I worked my way through endless variations—adjusting sugar, heat, how wide a pan I used, whether I soaked the fruit overnight, boiled it whole, cooked in anger or cooked with a friend—I began to realize something: *I wouldn't be enjoying this if it was easy.* I wouldn't be hooked if each batch was the same, if I didn't regret trekking uptown for bitter oranges or slicing up that one stupid pomelo.

Marmalade, and its constant proximity to success, has become a therapeutic gamble that fires my enthusiasm for the rare citric gems of the season and beats down my beliefs in myself at the same time. I've come to love the failures and heroic rescues as much as—or even more than—that one mysterious batch that worked right. And I've discovered there are two key ingredients that none of the recipes I've tried have ever listed: patience and faith. ○

Liz Clayton is a writer and photographer based in Brooklyn. Her work has appeared in Serious Eats, The Globe and Mail *and* The Yo La Tengo Gazette. *She published the book* Nice Coffee Time *in 2013.*

Read our recipe for Blood Orange and Bourbon Marmalade on page 142.

THE ART OF IMPROVISATION

WORDS BY MARGARET EVERTON & PHOTOGRAPH BY MAIA FLORE

If you forget your lines, sheet music or shopping list, chances are you'll have to act on the fly. Sometimes the best creations happen in the limbo between control and chaos, and learning how to harness that energy can help you triumph over life's unscripted moments.

Too cold to venture out around Strasbourg, food writer M.F.K. Fisher once famously cooked tangerines on the radiator. In a 1939 jam session, Charlie Parker realized he could melodically move to any key from the 12-tone chromatic scale, revolutionizing jazz soloing. When Monty Python couldn't afford horses for *The Holy Grail*, they clapped coconuts. History is rife with brilliant making-dos.

Improvisation can produce spontaneous masterpieces, but it makes people nervous. It's the black sheep of the road-to-results process, the tattooed wild child that makes its pedantic siblings *strategy* and *refinement* squirm. It often has a bad reputation for being erratic, flighty and undisciplined.

You don't need to suddenly embrace disorder or scatter laundry throughout your dwelling to benefit from acquiring what poet John Keats called "negative capability." Improvisation is the experience of residing in the uncomfortable and thrilling space of uncertainty that makes us feel euphoric and slightly light-headed. It lives within that fleeting moment when creativity wins out over tidy idleness.

Bona fide improv is an enigmatic creature that cannot be domesticated, only occasionally sighted. I can tell you what I've witnessed. One night, a man beside me at a dinner party generated hilarious limericks about misbehaving cats when given one-word prompts ("There once was a kitty from Kent…"). My grandmother drove through Texas for three weeks with just her underwear, a toothbrush and the dress on her back, picking up clothes from the thrift stores she chanced upon. I was once holed up during a Paris rainstorm with a roommate who pulled out the unpromising food remains from the fridge—leeks, lamb, haricots verts, flour, one soft potato, thyme—inspected them with folded arms and then assembled a kind of haute shepherd's pie. When the crust burned in the oven, she shrugged it off with another sip of good red. It actually added to the evening's charm, and I'll forever equate lightly charred food and Nina Simone's voice with a vague sense of well-being.

But let's not confuse impromptu living with recklessness. Uneducated improvisation is disconcerting: beginner dancers attacking the tango, an unlicensed driver, your roommate's experimental cocktail you're still trying to forget. Good improv is usually grounded in strict theory that becomes pliant when applied with a little creativity: You have to know the technique behind what you are trying to do, then depart from it. Think of how long a rock climber trains before winging it at 4,000 feet in a homemade harness or the number of canvases the Cubists filled before developing their own technique. Robert De Niro studied at two prestigious acting conservatories before rattling off *Taxi Driver*'s legendary "You talkin' to me?" mirror rant: The script simply directed him to talk to himself.

But why would we willingly subject ourselves to the discomfort of the unknown? Perhaps it's because the process of improvising makes us better people. John Cleese (of coconut-clapping fame) said that creativity is not a talent, but a way of operating. It refines how we face the uninvited surprises of life. Maybe your flight to Istanbul gets rerouted and you regroup. Perhaps you go through an unexpected breakup and find the way to move forward. Maybe your in-laws are suddenly in town and coming straight over, hungry. You may burn their dinner, but you'll shrug it off because you can fallibly and joyously make do with what you have. ○

Margaret Everton is an arts and culture writer and an explorer of how and what people create. She lives in Portland, Oregon, where she improvs French cuisine with mixed results.

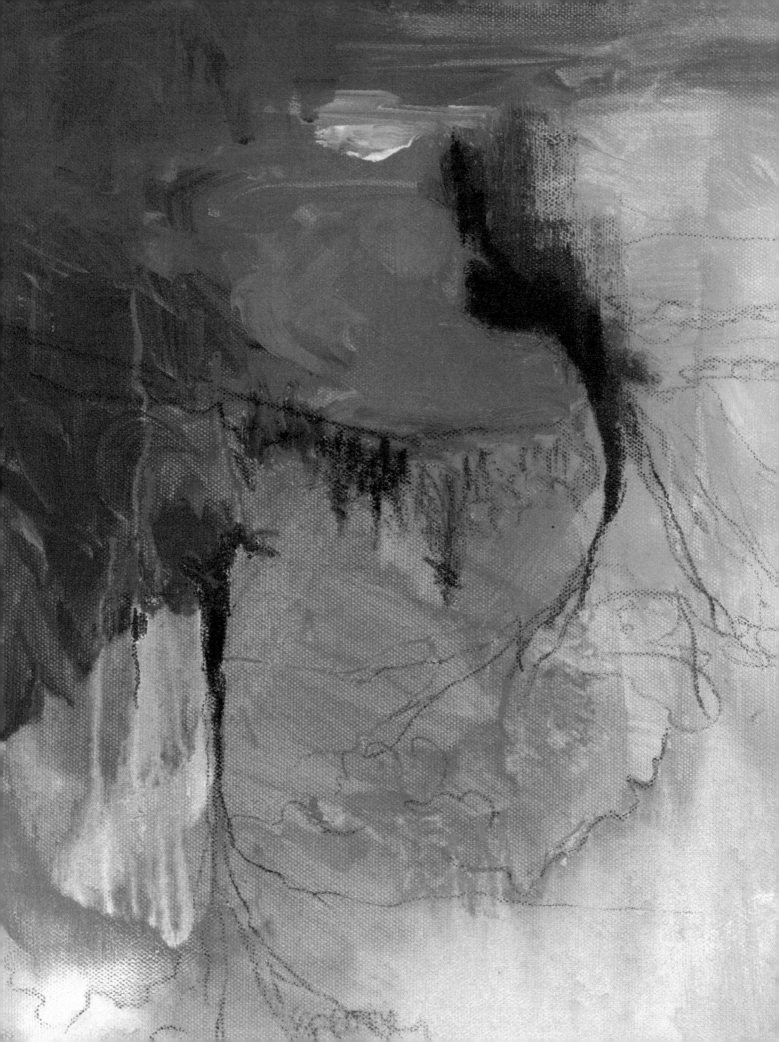

TWO

ENTERTAINING FOR TWO

○ ○

SEEING DOUBLE

PHOTOGRAPHS BY NEIL BEDFORD & ART DIRECTION BY CHARLOTTE HEAL
STYLING BY RACHEL CAULFIELD

Identical twins may appear to be perfect imitations of each other, but when you look closely at their mirrored reflections, their minute differences can reveal much more than mismatched freckles.

Despite what high school biology class may have led you to believe, identical twins aren't *actually* identical. Split from the same fertilized egg, though they theoretically share matching chromosomes and genomes, their DNA varies ever so slightly. And this isn't just to do with nurture's environmental influences, such as dad raising one to be a cross-country athlete and mom pushing the other into a life of professional violin playing: Nature also plays its role through a scientific phenomenon known as "genetic divergence." As a result, one twin may be a half-inch taller, have a different jawline or love the taste of aniseed while the other despises it. These minuscule differences are what make twins distinct individuals instead of carbon copies, giving them their own personalities, sympathies and opinions. To better understand this marvel, we photographed and interviewed a few pairs from London about their resemblances and distinctions.

—

TIDA AND LISA

HOW DO YOU DIFFER AS TWINS?

Lisa: Scientifically speaking, we are actually what are called "mirror twins," which occur in a small percentage of monozygotic twins [twins from the same egg] as a result of a late split of the eggs. This leads to opposite skills and characteristics: I'm right-handed and Tida is left-handed; I have a more dominant left brain and Tida has a more dominant right brain; I'm more logical and Tida is more creative. I think people are also shaped by nurture, knowledge and their environment though: The knowledge that I was born first probably led me to take on the protective older sister role, and then the knowledge of the mirror twin phenomenon has also played its part.

ANNA AND SONIA (LEFT)

WHAT LIKENESSES DO YOU SHARE?

Sonia: Physically we are quite similar, but mentally we are two different personas—sweet and sour. People always tend to compare our voices or our skills as if one has to be better than the other.

LINDSEY AND CARRIE (ABOVE)

WHAT'S THE DOWNSIDE OF BEING A TWIN?

Lindsey: Absolutely nothing, unless you count always being used as bookends to make school photos symmetrical, or having to share your birthday—there must have been some gift-related sulks when we were kids!

MEGAN AND KATHRYN (ABOVE)

ARE THERE DISADVANTAGES OF HAVING A TWIN?

Kathryn: Sometimes the advantages can be the disadvantages I suppose, like having someone there all the time. People also call us "the twins" rather than Megan and Kathryn, but I think that's changing as we get older.

CHARLOTTE AND ANOUK (PAGE 60)

HAVE YOU EVER HAD ANY STEREOTYPICAL TWIN EXPERIENCES?

Charlotte: When we were five, I fell and hit my head against the sharp edge of a table. It bled tremendously and our parents took me to the hospital to get it stitched, but I didn't cry at all while Anouk was crying and screaming!

THE EXTREMISTS' GUIDE TO HOME DECOR

Are you an obsessive hoarder or an ultra-purger? Here are a few tips for breaking out of your less-than-ideal decorating methods.

WORDS BY GAIL O'HARA &
ILLUSTRATIONS BY SARAH JACOBY

THE MINIMALISTS' GUIDE TO BULKING UP

TAKE A SEAT So you've been stalking an actual Eames Aluminum Group chair online, but you're not likely to have the money to buy it until 2023? Consider getting something else to sit on in the meantime. Your derriere will thank you.

ADVENTURES IN STEREO You went from compact discs to records to CDs in a binder to MP3s and now your entire media library fits in your shirt pocket. Congratulations, you have no stuff! Add the warm, joyful experience of turntable listening to your bucket list.

BLANK SLATE Empty frames are fine, but putting something in them might show a bit more personality. Of course, putting a nail through the wall might upset your fragile constitution (and release lead paint particles into your dust-free space), but wouldn't it be lovely to have something to stare at other than a dull white wall?

IN THE CLOSET Is your wardrobe so tiny, expensive and overly curated that you run out of things to wear every 72 hours? We give you permission to add a few things to your near-empty closet so you can spend less time at the laundromat.

THE ACQUISITIONISTS' GUIDE TO LETTING GO

HIDDEN PATHWAYS Some of us enjoy being surrounded by lots of wonderful stuff, but there are ways to get organized and add a bit of order to your enormous collections of photographs, broken tea cups and non-functioning 1960s Polaroid cameras. We'd recommend you go find a glass display case or a metal legal bookshelf at a thrift store, but we know you: You'll come home with *even more stuff*. Other options include hiding your precious cargo behind frosted Plexiglas room dividers or buying wonderful old card catalogs.

YOU'RE A KEEPER Being a collector is great. Creating art installations out of dirty dishes is less appealing. Perhaps you used to collect vintage jewelry boxes or porcelain hedgehogs, but just because your favorite cousin gifted you one of these items doesn't mean you have to hang on to it for life. Who knows what kind of glittering treasures you've stashed away that might translate into fast cash?

THE FRAME GAME Even if you're the proud owner of a ton of art, you don't need to hang every single piece up on the wall at once. Your home should be a well-curated gallery of only the most important mementos. And please, go easy on the taxidermied critters.

MEDIA LIBRARY If those vinyl records haven't been played in a year, consider a purge. Have a stoop sale, give some of those doubles away as gifts or donate them to local libraries and record stores. This goes for books too: If you aren't in love with it, leave it on a park bench or in a café for someone else to pick up.

YOUR BEST FOOT You haven't worn heels in a decade but you still have a museum-worthy collection of sparkly platforms, gilded Miu Miu knockoffs and other teetering pumps. Put them back into the world so that someone will actually wear them! Imagine being able to find your favorite pair of sneakers without looking through 29 boxes.

IMPERFECT PITCH

WORDS BY TRAVIS ELBOROUGH & PHOTOGRAPH BY ANJA VERDUGO
STYLING BY ALISON BRISLIN

Achieving perfection in music is all but impossible, short of an auto-tuner. We look back at the pops and cracks that have made music interesting.

The 17th-century violins built by Antonio Stradivari are virtually synonymous with musical perfection, but scientists have suggested their flaws make them sound superior—their distinct tone can be attributed to centuries of botched repairs. Similarly, if we look at the history of pop, it's the imperfections that have often added to the score of musical experience.

1950s: THE ROUGH ROUTE TO ROCK & ROLL The clattery drums on Bill Haley's "Rock Around the Clock," whose opening snare-beat snap served as a starting pistol for rock & roll, were caused by the producer rushing the mix. Because the song was the B-side, he left it rough to devote more time to the A-side, but the song's raw imperfection proved infectious to the first generation of disc-flippers.

1960s: BUM NOTE SAMBA Fed up with accompanying a tone-deaf nightclub singer, Newton Mendonça and legendary "The Girl From Ipanema" songwriter Antonio Carlos Jobim composed the mocking "Desafinado" (meaning "out of key") in revenge. As fiendishly difficult to sing as it was catchy, it started the bossa nova boom, making bad singing the creative catalyst for some truly beautiful Brazilian music.

1960s: A MONARCH MISTAKE Portland, Oregon's the Kingsmen are known for their famed cover of a single song, "Louie, Louie." A primal blast of '60s garage rock that was recorded in a single take, it was rendered all the more thrilling by singer Jack Ely fluffing a verse.

1970s: STRIKE THREE CHORDS Bored of the virtuoso excesses of progressive groups in the 1970s, the punk ethos said to learn three chords and form a band. No longer needing to play properly, people were free to create as they saw fit, encouraging millions to pick up instruments and have a go.

1980s & '90s: ERROR TO EDM The Roland 808 was a drum machine whose timing was deemed so erratic and sounded so unlike real drums that its own manufacturer took it off the market in 1983. Later snapped up cheap by bedroom techno pioneers who cherished its idiosyncrasies, it became the heartbeat of rap, rave and dance music.

2000s: TUNE-UP Here is the concrete proof that perfection is not always welcome in music. The pitch correction software Auto-Tune has all but banished singing out of key—on record and even live in concert. But the result is that almost any recording it's used on sounds robotically, monotonously, boringly similar.

2010s: SMASHING DISCS The recent decade has seen a revival of vinyl records: Could this be some sign of a deep yearning for scuzzy imperfection in an age of immaculate digital reproduction? The thing about physical records is that the very process of playing them leaves them less-perfect objects. A little needle-wear enriches them: A minor scratch on a much-loved single or LP turns a mass-produced item into a singular personal object. Far from ruining it, that scratch adds something to each listen that no other copy has. Sometimes the worse the imperfection, the closer to perfect it sounds. ○ ○

Travis Elborough is the author of The Vinyl Countdown: The Album from LP to iPod and Back Again *(Soft Skull Press) and owns four records by the Kingsmen.*

INTERVIEW

RAISING THE BARRE

The world of ballet is full of high-flying heartache as dancers strive for a perfection they know doesn't exist. New York City Ballet's Wendy Whelan talks to us about the challenges and triumphs of a 30-year career.

WORDS BY GEORGIA FRANCES KING & PHOTOGRAPH BY JOSS MCKINLEY

Ballerinas are some of the toughest folks around: Not only can they balance their slender bodies on surface areas the size of a matchbook, suspend gravity's existence and have the cerebral strength of a hot coal walker, but they'll also destroy you in a chin-up competition. Ballet is known for being one of the most difficult creative endeavors you can pursue—both physically and mentally—and the pressure to be the very embodiment of perfection is extreme. Wendy Whelan knows it better than most: After 30 years with the New York City Ballet, she'll take her final curtsy with the company at the end of this year, off to pursue the world of contemporary dance. A passionate and spirited woman, she has managed to avoid the shackles of a career path that has the ability to crush spirits in the same way that pointe shoes crunch toes. We spoke with her on her 47th birthday about the changing face of perfection and what only time can tell.

A TEACHER ONCE SAID YOU WEREN'T A PRODIGY, AND YOU SAID THAT WAS A BLESSING. WHY?

As an adult, I know that perfection doesn't exist. As a kid, I didn't know that yet. When my teacher told me I wasn't a prodigy, I said, "But I want to be one!" However, I also knew that *he* knew I had the strength of character, the heart and the passion, and those would carry me toward success. He was right. The challenges have been a huge source of motivation for me, and I was happier having to put in the extra work in the end. I know a lot of prodigies now, and it's not easy for them to stay challenged.

ON TOP OF COPING WITH PRESSURE CONCERNING YOUR APPEARANCE, WEIGHT, HEIGHT AND EVERYTHING ELSE SUPERFICIAL, YOU WERE ALSO QUIETLY DEALING WITH A SERIOUS BONE DISORDER, SCOLIOSIS. HOW DID YOUR TWISTED SPINE AFFECT YOUR APPROACH TO DANCE?

When I was 12 years old, I pulled a hamstring and went to an orthopedist who discovered what was going on. He did a scoliosis check and said, "Wow, you have quite a curve in your back." After his diagnosis, I spent my summer in the hospital lying in a traction device for a week at a time—I grew an inch and a half in that first week. Then I was put in a body cast from my shoulders to my hips for a month, then back into the hospital to be in traction again. I thought I'd have to take the summer off because I had to wear this 15-pound plaster body cast, but my teachers—who luckily were so forward-thinking—said, "You know, you're doing so well right now that we don't want you to stop. You should come in and do whatever you can do with your limitations. Just lift your leg as high as it can go." It wasn't going to go very high, but because of that, I could focus on other aspects of my dancing.

HOW DID YOUR PHYSICAL RESTRICTIONS HELP YOU MENTALLY?

Because of my limitation, I could focus on the smaller ideas that are built into the bigger ones: So if I couldn't work on how high my leg could go, then I'd focus on my turn-out instead. I could work on things I wouldn't necessarily notice otherwise, and my technique really improved in the end. That particular summer really shaped my character and the way I think about the power of limitation.

HOW MUCH OF BALLET IS MENTAL AND HOW MUCH IS PHYSICAL?

The mental and physical challenges are what make ballet interesting to a dancer. Jumping those hurdles and pushing yourself every day gets the endorphins going in your body, it gets energy going, it's exciting, it's thrilling! The whole point of striving for excellence and perfection is that you see improvement from all the work you're putting in and that just feeds itself more and more.

Sometimes I feel like it's akin to meditation: You can reach this point of purity that's blissful and potentially heavenly. To get there, to actually feel it and to know that it exists in your humanness is such a profound thing. *That* is what we're actually striving for with all of our work. I once said there are no perfect dancers, but there are moments of perfection within a dance. Those moments are fleeting, but when you feel them, it's such incredible bliss.

HOW HAS YOUR AGE AFFECTED YOUR MENTALITY TOWARD YOUR CRAFT?

Today's actually my 47th birthday! I'm trying to find ways to refocus my artistry so it fits with where I'm at in life right now and the strengths I'm gaining and the strengths I'm losing. I don't have to stay the same. People may come to recognize a "special dancer," but eventually the body will begin to age and certain strengths will be lost—physical powers that will never be regained. Time doesn't stop, but that doesn't mean you can't keep evolving. I don't want to deny the changes that are happening: I want to continue to move forward with them, appreciate them, love them and make beauty out of them.

WHAT ARE YOU TRYING TO ACHIEVE WITH DELVING INTO CONTEMPORARY DANCE THROUGH YOUR NEW PROJECT, *RESTLESS CREATURE*?

I was never typically the most classical of ballet dancers. I've always been drawn toward more angular and abstract things, and I wanted to follow that to the next level. I'm really using *Restless Creature* as an exploration for where I can go. It's time for a transformation, and with that, I don't mind that my body will shift into new ways of moving anymore. I'm interested to see what my body does—where strength will build, where weight will fall and how I'll adjust to that and find inspiration from it.

IS BALLET MORE DIFFICULT THAN CONTEMPORARY DANCE?

It's very different. For me, the main challenge is going from the balletic idea of being ephemeral and light and off the ground to finding my weight and connection with the ground. In ballet you're trying to be this untouchable ideal, but in modern and contemporary dance I feel my imperfections are more welcomed. It's a different way of connecting with your body. I really want to work in more intimate environments, I want to work closer to my audience, and I want to be touchable.

YOU SPEND SO MUCH TIME CHASING PERFECTION PROFESSIONALLY, BUT WHAT AREAS OF YOUR LIFE ARE TOTALLY, UTTERLY IMPERFECT?

So many things! I don't cook, I can't sing… You don't have to be good at everything: Choose what you love and focus your life around that. That'll bring such satisfaction. So what if you'll never be able to roast the perfect chicken! There are plenty of other parts of your life where you can find success.

HOW HAVE YOU LEARNED TO CELEBRATE YOUR OWN IMPERFECTIONS?

My husband has played a pivotal role in that. He's a visual artist and has given me a lot of ideas about perfection. He finds such beauty in people's imperfections, and I'm so fascinated by that because we're all filled with them. Everybody sees themselves differently: I see my crooked back, my crooked teeth and my differences. When I was younger, I didn't know where I was going to find my own unique beauty, but now I've found so much of it in my imperfections. ○ ○

After 30 years of dancing with the New York City Ballet, Wendy Whelan will step down this fall to perform Restless Creature, *a suite of four duets touring the US in 2015. Visit wendywhelan.com for more details.*

MAKING A POINTE

*Prima ballerina Wendy Whelan offers some words of advice based on
what she has learned while sashaying through her dancing career.*

PHOTOGRAPHS BY BERTIL NILSSON

KEEP AN OPEN MIND Growing up in Louisville, Kentucky—of all places—I had three very different ideas of ballet being taught to me at the same time: the Paris Opera Ballet School, the Royal Ballet School and the Maggie Black study of dance. Eventually, I moved to New York to focus solely on the George Balanchine [the charismatic father of modern American ballet] style. A teacher would say, "This is the only way to do this step," and then in the next class another teacher would say, "No, *this* is the way to do this step." I enjoyed the challenge of committing to each different idea with each instructor—by working within this melting pot of styles, I could find my true identity as a dancer. I see a real strength and beauty in appreciating all the different approaches.

FIND YOUR UNIQUENESS When I was a younger dancer in the 1970s, there was a strong aesthetic for long and lean and thin in ballet—a "model-like" beauty. It was intimidating to try and fit that exact body type, but over time I've seen that idea soften. The world has opened up its eyes to different kinds of bodies dancing ballet—there isn't a certain look or "one way" anymore. People aren't comparing themselves to each other as much, and that's really healthy. It's up to the dancer herself to find what is special within her, whether it's her strength, her musculature, her thinness, her delicacy, her softness or her hardness. You have to ask, "*What is it that's special about me?*" and take that, make it work, play with it, and see what you can do with it.

MAKE IT YOUR OWN One thing Balanchine's philosophy has taught me is to keep moving forward and not stay locked in to a certain box of ideas. He cast different body types in the same roles to shine light on the complexities of his choreography and to see the same steps danced differently. When passing down a role, some teachers want you to dance a role the way Balanchine told them to dance it. But I also believe that he wanted honesty and truth and life in his ballets, so he would want for it to be *you* more than anything. Whenever I pass down a role, I tell the new ballerina everything I know about the piece, but I will always encourage her to make it her own—that's really the only way to bring out the true essence of a dance.

BE ADAPTABLE Dancers know how to recover quickly when they fall: Whether it's in class or during a performance, we always find a way to stand up and keep going. A powerful generation of great 20th-century choreographers has now passed away: Balanchine, Frederick Ashton, Kenneth MacMillan, Jerome Robbins, Martha Graham and Merce Cunningham. Without their presence, things have definitely changed, but we owe it to them to take their ideas and move forward with the momentum of what's happening today. Nothing we do is ever really perfect because it's constantly changing. One thing I learned a long time ago that I continue to believe in today is this: "The only thing perfect in life is perfectly dead."

PRACTICE MAKES PERFECT You can only become a great artist by striving every day with rigor for perfection. When I was at the School of American Ballet, there were some very old-school Russian teachers. They were really hard-core, and I absolutely loved them for that. They were teaching us to strive for perfection. They probably knew that it didn't really exist, but it's in that idea of striving for it where so much of our beauty lies: It pulls at the mind, the heart and the body. The beautiful art of ballet would be dead if our teachers didn't ask us to show them perfection. Within that struggle, every once in a while you'll hit on it, and it's just gorgeous. As ballet dancers, we live our lives trying to come by those moments of grace. ○ ○

WHEN LIFE GIVES YOU LEMONS...

... drink tequila. This boozy cocktail and mood-lifting dinner duo features the sourest member of the citrus family and will turn that puckered face into a smile.

RECIPES BY DIANA YEN
PHOTOGRAPHS BY JIM GOLDEN & STYLING BY KARYN FIEBICH

LEMON TEQUILA PALOMA WITH ROSEMARY AND GINGER

Kosher salt, for dipping

2 lemon wedges

1/4 cup (60 milliliters) fresh lemon juice

2 tablespoons Rosemary Ginger Simple Syrup

1 sprig fresh rosemary

1/4 cup (60 milliliters) tequila

1/4 cup (60 milliliters) sparkling water

Candied ginger, for garnish

- - -

METHOD Place the salt in a shallow dish. Rub the rim of a glass with a lemon wedge, dip the rim in the salt and fill with ice. Put the lemon juice, a lemon wedge, the Rosemary Ginger Simple Syrup and the fresh rosemary into a cocktail shaker and muddle. Add ice and the tequila and shake. Strain into the salt-rimmed glass filled with ice and top off with the sparkling water. Garnish the glass with a lemon wedge and the candied ginger on a pick.

Serves 1

ROSEMARY GINGER SIMPLE SYRUP

1 cup (225 grams) sugar

1 cup (235 milliliters) water

5 sprigs fresh rosemary

2 5-inch pieces of ginger (about 4 ounces/115 grams), cut into thin rounds

- - -

METHOD Bring the sugar and water to a boil in a saucepan. Continue stirring until the sugar dissolves. Remove from the heat. Add the rosemary and ginger and let steep for 30 minutes. Pour the syrup through a sieve into an airtight container. Refrigerate until ready to use.

Makes about 1 1/4 cups

LEMON ARUGULA RICOTTA RAVIOLI
WITH BROWN BUTTER AND CRISPY SAGE

FOR THE PASTA DOUGH:

3 1/2 cups (590 grams)
all-purpose flour

5 large eggs

1 teaspoon extra-virgin olive oil

1/2 teaspoon salt

FOR THE FILLING:

1 1/2 cups (340 grams)
fresh ricotta cheese

3 tablespoons lemon zest

1 teaspoon fresh lemon juice

1/4 cup (55 grams) grated
Parmesan cheese

1 tablespoon unsalted butter

5 cups (130 grams) arugula

Salt and pepper, to taste

FOR THE SAUCE:

1/2 cup (110 grams)
unsalted butter

8 sage leaves, torn

A pinch of salt

FOR MAKING THE RAVIOLI:

All-purpose flour
for the work surface

1 large egg, beaten

METHOD Make the pasta dough: Mound the flour in the center of a clean work surface. Create a well in the middle and add the eggs, oil and salt. Using a fork, beat together the wet ingredients and begin to incorporate the flour, starting with the inner rim of the well. Work all of the flour into the eggs and then begin kneading the dough. Knead for 8 minutes, or until it looks smooth on the surface. Form the dough into a disk, wrap in plastic and allow to rest for 30 minutes at room temperature.

Make the arugula ricotta filling: In a mixing bowl, combine the ricotta, lemon zest, lemon juice and Parmesan. Over medium heat, melt the butter in a large skillet and then add the arugula. Stirring often, cook the greens until they begin to wilt, about 2 minutes. Remove from the heat and allow to cool. Roughly chop the arugula and add to the ricotta mixture. Season with salt and pepper to taste.

Make the sauce: Heat the butter, torn sage and salt in a large skillet over medium-high heat until aromatic and browned, about 3–5 minutes, or when the sage is crispy. Set aside and warm before serving.

Make the ravioli: Cut the fresh pasta dough lengthwise into 8 pieces on a lightly floured surface. Working one piece at a time, pass the dough through a pasta machine on the widest setting, starting at "1." Fold the dough in half and pass through again, slowly creating a rectangular shape. Continue passing through the machine, adjusting the setting higher each time until the desired thickness (1/8 inch) is reached. Dust the fresh pasta sheets with flour and drape over a rolling pin or pasta rack until ready to use. (If you don't have a pasta machine, roll out the pasta dough with a rolling pin to 1/8-inch thickness on a floured surface. Dust the sheets with flour and hang to dry until ready to use.)

ASSEMBLE Cut the pasta sheets into 2 1/2-inch-wide strips. Brush one strip lightly with the egg mixture. Leaving a 1/2-inch border around the edges, place about 1 teaspoon of the arugula ricotta filling at 1-inch intervals down the strip of dough. Lay another strip of dough over the first. Use your fingers to press and seal around each mound of filled dough. Use a knife or fluted pastry wheel to cut out the individual square of ravioli. Repeat with the remaining dough and filling.

Bring a large pot of salted water to a boil. Boil the ravioli in batches for about 2 minutes each until they float to the top. Use a slotted spoon to remove the ravioli from the boiling water.

Serve with the brown butter sauce and the crispy sage. ○ ○

Serves 4

THE AWKWARD PARTS

We all had childhood hang-ups that made us feel less than normal, whether it was
orthopedic shoes, an unfortunately placed birthmark or a caterpillar-like monobrow.
We revisit some of these so-called imperfections to see how they might benefit our adult lives.

WORDS BY GAIL O'HARA & ILLUSTRATIONS BY KATRIN COETZER

SEEING WITH FOUR EYES As a child you were ridiculed for your purply pink plastic frames with bottle-thick lenses, but as a grown-up you have the ability to become one of the world's foremost abstract painters. Simply removing your glasses means you can see landscapes in all their blurry, Monet-esque glory and re-create them in smears of oil paint.

SHOWING YOUR SPOTS You loathed your splattered speckled freckles when you were younger, but now you've learned to appreciate the way you can trace lines between them on your arms and legs and learn about constellations at the same time. Being spotty also means you can camouflage yourself in a pile of leaves or on your hikes into the jungle.

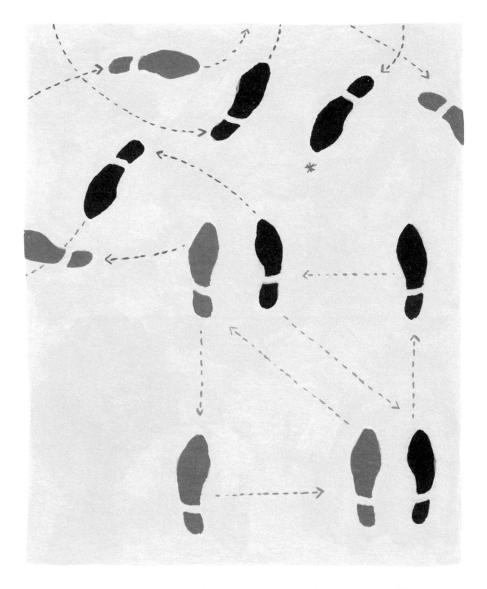

LACKING COORDINATION You were known for slapstick comedy and incessantly falling down as a wee thing, but now it's time to channel your lack of coordination into some manic, avant-garde interpretive moves by starting a new dance craze. Dance! Just like Elaine from *Seinfeld*. This super-clumsy tendency also means that none of your friends will ever ask you to help them move.

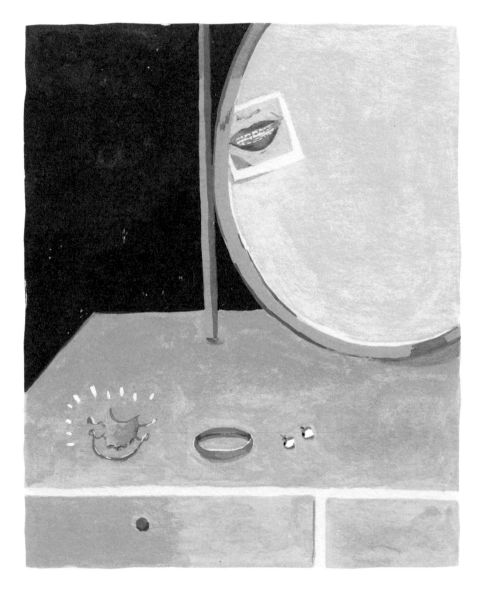

BEING A BRACE-FACE Kids sporting headgear once had their wires peppered with forgotten Cheerios or fretted constantly about being struck by lightning. But if you happen to be lost on a mountaintop, now you can flash your metal grin and help will arrive! And if it doesn't, the blinding glare could frighten the bears. Other benefits include the ability to gnaw away at ropes when you're tied up by bad guys and shoot rubber bands (gently) at the ill-behaved children you're babysitting.

HAVING HUMONGOUS HAIR Perhaps your classmates didn't appreciate the wonder of the gloriously voluminous hair you inherited. But your huge mane is now an asset that will keep you toasty during polar vortexes, help you smuggle snacks into the cinema and allow you to hide among the weeping willows should you come upon an angry pit bull. Additional benefits include creating ropes to exit the castle you're trapped in and leaving pillows at home when camping. ○ ○

GOING ROGUE

Despite your best intentions and laminated tour itineraries, no amount of planning will prevent unexpected mishaps while traveling. When disaster inevitably strikes, the best thing to do is revel in your newfound off-road freedom.

PHOTOGRAPHS BY WE ARE THE RHOADS & STYLING BY JENN BONNETT

HOW TO BE NEIGHBORLY: IMPERFECT NEIGHBORS

WORDS BY GEORGIA FRANCES KING & PHOTOGRAPH BY MARTIN WUNDERWALD

Sharing walls, floors and fences with strangers can make for some seriously cringe-worthy situations. If worst comes to worst, just ask yourself: What would Ned Flanders do?

WHEN YOU CAN HEAR YOUR NEIGHBOR SNEEZE (OR WORSE) If you live in an old building, creaky floorboards and paper-thin walls are sadly part of the draw. Unless your neighbor is harboring a clip-cloppy cowboy boot collection (complete with spurs), teaching tap-dancing classes at 11 p.m. on a Tuesday or singing Bon Jovi in the shower, it's best to put up with it and be considerate yourself. But if you must protest, gently trot upstairs to remind them of the importance of area rugs or suggest a shoe closet for the hallway. Broom handles banging on ceilings will leave marks as well as resentment.

WHEN THE GARBAGE IS CONSTANTLY OVERFLOWING If the recycling is full of moving boxes and IKEA-branded cardboard, hope that it'll stop once the new folks have settled. If it's full of empty wine bottles, consider dropping by on a Friday evening to "help out." If you can't beat them, join them.

WHEN THEY'RE STEALING YOUR INTERNET/VEGGIE BOX/PACKAGES The only thing worse than a thief is the one who strikes before you even have the brief joy of possession. Some people regard unguarded hallway packages like spare dinner rolls on a room service tray. So if there's someone you trust who's at home every day, have your parcels delivered to them in exchange for freshly baked goods.

WHEN THEY WANT TO CHAT (ALL THE TIME) There are limits when it comes to hallway banter: Safe topics are the weather, rent hikes and window-box gardens. Unsafe topics include gossiping about the neighbors or the landlord's choice of aftershave. Need to slip away? Mention you've left the kettle on or have to take a call soon, regardless of if you own a stove-top kettle or a landline (who does nowadays?).

WHEN YOU CAN SEE INTO THEIR APARTMENT Your bedroom window might overlook your neighbor's curtainless bathroom. Do they know? Do they care? Many people who live in shoeboxes have made peace with unintentional public nudity, so maybe it's you that needs to shut the blinds. And remember: If you can see them, they can see you too. Better polish your awkward smile and wave.

WHEN THEY HAVE A RAUCOUS PARTY AND KEEP YOU UP ALL NIGHT You often lie in bed wishing the commotion would stop but don't do anything to address it in the moment; an angry knock on the door the next morning won't make up for those lost hours of sleep. So pull on your bathrobe and say something. Even if they don't pipe down, at least you'll return to bed, helplessly awake, knowing you tried.

WHEN *YOU* HAVE A RAUCOUS PARTY AND KEEP *THEM* UP ALL NIGHT If you know in advance you'll be making noise, pop notes under everyone's doors, warning them about the festivities and inviting them along: They can't be as angry if you've asked them to join. And suggest that they call you instead of the cops: Better to have the disgruntled elderly lady from 4C on your case than a SWAT team. ○ ○

Georgia Frances King is the editor of Kinfolk *and has always had a splendid relationship with her landlord (the secret is edible bribes). Growing up in Melbourne, Australia, she now lives in Portland, Oregon.*

PROFILE SERIES

BEST IN SHOW

WORDS BY GEORGIA FRANCES KING

PHOTOGRAPHS BY CHARLIE SCHUCK & STYLING BY LAUREN COLTON

We interview a Westminster Dog Show judge, an Olympic gymnastics adjudicator and a Pulitzer Prize–winning food critic about whether it's possible to ever accurately judge perfection.

JONATHAN GOLD: Pulitzer Prize–winning restaurant critic, Los Angeles, California

THE HON. DAVID C. MERRIAM: 2015 Westminster Best in Show judge, Bonsall, California

CHERYL HAMILTON: Olympic women's gymnastics judge, Newark, Delaware

---

P rofessional judging is a peculiar concept. It's programmed into our neural pathways to divide and conquer information, ranking and ordering it just so. We're not satisfied with sampling three *pains au chocolat* and saying they're all equally tasty, or listening to a few of our favorite albums without mentally categorizing our whole discography. We yearn for hierarchy. We crave conclusive certainty. And we seek out the opinions of certified adjudicators to give authority to our judgmental whims.

These judges are tasked with the seemingly impossible charge of not only determining quality, but also the ability to definitively set apart nearly identical examples of excellence. What factors come in to play when separating a brilliant two–Michelin star restaurant from the Herculean three? Are you better off poorly executing a challenging back-uprise-straddle-cut-to-L on the parallel bars or flawlessly landing a simpler handspring-front-salto on vault? And how could you possibly size up a yappy Pomeranian against a grand Dalmatian? In the end, each of these worlds comes with its own set of standards for determining a winner between many near-perfect entities.

Though their subject matter varies from Dobermans to desserts and double-pikes, our three interview subjects could all agree on one thing: Perfection is arbitrary, but despite that knowledge, we strive for it anyway. And that's what these judges truly judge: the glorious pursuit of an unattainable goal.

THE CULINARY JUDGE

In a time when public online reviews are holding their own against Michelin stars, there remain few trusted arbiters of taste. Esteemed Los Angeles Times *restaurant critic Jonathan Gold is the only writer to have won a Pulitzer Prize for a piece of food criticism, and enjoys a professional life filled with ghee, analogies and hole-in-the-wall ethnic cuisine. While ranking restaurants for a living may sound like a delightfully breezy occupation, he tells us about the challenges of measuring one bratwurst's might against another.*

ARE THERE ANY RULES WHEN IT COMES TO CULINARY CRITIQUING?

The rules of criticism are the same whether you're reviewing a meal, a film or a book of philosophy: It's the critic's responsibility to approach the object of review with an open mind, an honest curiosity, a reasonable understanding of context, and to put in the necessary homework.

WHO SETS THE STANDARDS FOR WHAT'S CONSIDERED "GOOD FOOD"? ARE THEY DICTATED BY CRITICS, CHEFS, THE PUBLIC OR AN ARBITRARY SET OF CULTURAL CODES?

Good food is good food: The entity identifying it as such is irrelevant. That said, somebody who has tasted crème brûlée at 200 restaurants is generally better equipped to assess number 201 than a novice encountering the numbingly rich dessert for the first time, and is also better equipped to put the dish in its cultural context. Is the more experienced person often a critic? Indeed.

CAN GOOD TASTE BE TAUGHT, OR IS IT AN INTUITIVE QUALITY?

A scientist friend, the late Seymour Benzer of Caltech, spent the last decade of his life working on the genetic basis of taste. Through gene-splicing, he raised a strain of fruit flies that were attracted to wasabi, a taste they ordinarily loathe. His theory was that we're born with our preferences, and I largely agree with him. But any of us can certainly learn to appreciate nuances and build up a sophisticated bank of taste memory— a kind of culinary literacy.

HOW DO YOU APPROACH THE SUBJECTIVE NOTION OF CRITIQUING FOOD?

Is it subjective? Because if I have developed firmly held ideas about what a Mysore dosa should be—including crispness, tang of fermentation, pliability, porousness, density of filling and size—then any Mysore dosa I encounter is measured against that ideal. But what if my ideal is different from yours? Do I automatically dismiss a soggy, overstuffed San Francisco Mission burrito just because it's not one of the crisp, modest, spicy East L.A. burritos I prefer? Of course not. Part of the process is absorbing the aesthetic from which a dish arises, then attempting to evaluate it on its own terms. I may state preferences on occasion, but I'm not a cultural supremacist. I've returned to some restaurants more than a dozen times in an attempt to understand their cuisine.

HOW DOES YOUR PERSONAL TASTE INFLUENCE YOUR REVIEW? HOW HARD IS IT TO REMAIN OBJECTIVE?

My preferences may enter into the way I review a restaurant, but I'd like to think that I can recognize a brilliant example of something I don't particularly like. I loathe poached eggs, for an example, but I know the difference between a good one and a bad one.

WHAT ARE YOUR THOUGHTS ON CULINARY JUDGING COMPETITIONS SUCH AS THE JAMES BEARD AWARDS?

The Beards, the San Pellegrino Top 50 and the like often come off as arbitrary—it's all but impossible for one person to eat at enough restaurants across the country (or the world) to be able to make a reasoned judgment. But the awards do no harm and people seem to like them. At the *Los Angeles Times*, I put together an annual list of the 101 best restaurants in the region, ranked in order, and it gets more attention than anything I do all year. It's fun.

WHAT'S THE DIFFERENCE BETWEEN A FOUR AND A FOUR-AND-A-HALF STAR RESTAURANT?

I've never given stars. They tend to indicate a restaurant's category rather than its quality, and I have no interest in that.

DOES THE PERFECT MEAL EXIST?

I'd like to think so, though I've never experienced such a thing.

WHEN DOES IMPERFECTION HAVE A PLACE IN FINE DINING?

Imperfection in a great meal means that the chef is striving for something different. Out of the 30-odd plates over the course of a tasting dinner at Pierre Gagnaire, my favorite restaurant in Paris, three or four may be totally off. This somehow makes the other ones even better.

ARE THERE ANY FOOD TRENDS OTHER PEOPLE LOVE AND YOU DESPISE, OR VICE VERSA?

I'm often accused of an undue fascination with offal, which is perhaps true, as well as foraged herbs, unusual seafood, well-raised meat and stinky natural wines. I'll be delighted when the egg-on-everything craze dies down, and I see no need to ever eat another kale salad.

YOU WORKED IN MUSIC JOURNALISM BEFORE MOVING INTO FOOD: WHAT ARE THE DIFFERENCES BETWEEN THE TWO?

Music is more abstract than food, and a critic needs to work a bit harder to put it into context. Still, in a way, music and cooking both rise out of pop culture, and it seems as if I engage the same faculties when writing about either.

HOW DOES YOUR EXACTING MIND-SET FACTOR INTO OTHER AREAS OF YOUR LIFE?

I've been a critic of classical music, pop, theater, movies, art and books. I was once asked to write a column about love, and I refused. I wanted at least one part of my life to remain unexamined.

NOW THAT IT'S YOUR LIVELIHOOD, DO YOU ENJOY EATING OUT MORE OR LESS?

I've been writing about food professionally for about 30 years. I've completely lost the ability to sit down to a meal without thinking critically about it, and I could probably write 2,500 words a week about the toast I make every morning.

WHAT HAS FOOD CRITICISM TAUGHT YOU ABOUT OTHER AREAS OF LIFE?

It's okay to stop when you are full.

THE BEST IN SHOW JUDGE

The Hon. David C. Merriam, a considerate man in his seventies who spent decades on the bench as a California State Trials judge, has spent a lifetime adjudicating both canines and criminals. While the law may seem less capricious than the glossiness of a dog's coat, David maintains that the two worlds are quite alike. An international expert on bull terriers, he'll be judging his first Best in Show for the 2015 Westminster Kennel Club Dog Show. He tells us about what goes through his mind as he's sizing up our four-legged friends.

WHAT INTERESTED YOU ABOUT DOG JUDGING?

Things that influence you when you're young affect the way you spend your whole life. I've had this built-in bias since I was 14 years old. If I'd gotten interested in cats, I suppose I'd have done the same thing with cats! The amazing thing about our society is that we develop a subculture for whatever interest there is. Americans like competition of almost any nature: Whether it's baton twirling, dog breeding or off-road racing, we don't just *do* them—they're organized.

WOULD YOU PLEASE EXPLAIN THE FOUNDATION FOR DOG SHOW JUDGING?

Any judging involves two factors: one, a standard, and two, the evaluation of an object in comparison to that standard. With the American Kennel Club, which is the body that governs US dog showing and breeding, the standard is written to define the ideal specimen of each breed, and then we judge each dog against its breed standard.

HOW IS THE WRITTEN STANDARD FOR THE PERFECT BREED SPECIMEN DETERMINED, AND HOW HAS IT CHANGED WITH TIME?

They vary from breed to breed. For an example, the sporting dogs' standard specifies the physical characteristics of the function they were bred for, but the standards have evolved since they were first set in the early 19th century, and most breeds have moved away from function into what the breeders of the day think is aesthetically pleasing. Not many standards change very quickly though, so there's a fair amount of continuity.

CAN YOU PLEASE GIVE US SOME EXAMPLES OF THE AREAS COVERED IN THOSE BREED STANDARDS?

They start out with General Appearance, and those are sometimes amusing. They may chauvinistically describe the ideal specimen as having "great heart and courage." And, well, you can't judge that! Those are the historic remains of breed descriptions and aren't really important when you're judging anymore: Now you get down to the details of size, proportion, head, forequarters, hindquarters, coat, color, movement and things of that nature.

THE BEST IN BREED WINNERS ADVANCE TO BEST IN GROUP (DIVIDED INTO SPORTING, WORKING, TERRIER, HOUND, TOY, HERDING AND NON-SPORTING BREEDS), AND THOSE SEVEN WINNERS THEN COMPETE FOR BEST IN SHOW. HOW DO YOU JUDGE SEVEN VERY DIFFERENT DOGS AGAINST EACH OTHER?

In theory it's very understandable: You judge how close the boxer is to the boxer standard versus how close the standard poodle is to the standard poodle standard. We're not looking for the perfect dog, but the *best* one according to the breed standard. So the first question is: Does the Best in Show judge know nearly 180 varieties of breeds well enough do that? Really, judging is knowledge. And the other question is: Do the judges have the ability to accurately judge that dog in the two and a half minutes they're given to evaluate? Maybe computers could do it perfectly, but human beings can't—they just do it as well as they can.

HOW HARD IS IT TO REMAIN OBJECTIVE?

There's a subjectivity involved that doesn't exist in, say, horse racing, where the one who's there first wins. One can read the standard and say, "Okay, they're not supposed to be more than 20 inches at the withers and have a coat that's more than 2 inches in length," but there are two other important aspects of judging a breed: type, and soundness in body and mind. Only lastly do you look at what most of the spectators look at in a dog show, and that's showmanship. It's an aspect with a dog show because you have to be able to *show*, but it's not as important as type and soundness.

HOW DO YOU BECOME QUALIFIED TO JUDGE BEST IN SHOW ACROSS ALL SEVEN BREED TYPES?

You have to keep applying to be qualified to judge more breeds, and that means judging a great deal. I've been in the sport for well over 60 years and have spent many thousands of hours at dog shows. You can watch me doing Westminster and think, "What in the world is going through his mind?" I certainly know more about bull terriers than basset hounds!

ARE THE HANDLERS AND JUDGES REALLY AS CRAZED AS THEY ARE IN *BEST IN SHOW*?

Of course they are! It's a subculture of our society that has all the quirks and idiosyncrasies that every other one does. If you want to win, and you're against good, strong competition, then there is the joy of victory and the agony of defeat. Any activity that can't step back, relax and look at its own idiosyncrasies, faults and strange ways of acting is a little too uptight.

HOW HAS THE INDUSTRY BEEN APPROACHING THE ETHICAL AMBIGUITIES OF PUREBRED HEALTH PROBLEMS AND DOG INBREEDING?

There have been two approaches. The Kennel Club in England has begun to include health characteristics as part of their judging procedures. The judge is supposed to say, "This dog is not healthy because its nasal passages are obstructed, or its legs are of such a nature that the dog can't walk as it ought to walk." Whereas the American approach is to develop tests for determining genetic defects at the breeder level in order to try and eliminate the bad qualities and move the good qualities forward. We give the breeders the tools so they can fix a genetic problem within their breed.

WHAT DID YOU LEARN IN COURT THAT YOU'VE APPLIED TO DOG JUDGING?

Dog show judging is much the same as judging in the courts of law—it's a universal principle. Concentration is probably important, and of course there's the question of integrity. It's terribly important in our codes of sportsmanship that you judge only the dogs and you don't let any other factors or biases interfere. But the courts weren't competitive: The dog part is competition.

THE OLYMPIC GYMNASTICS JUDGE

Whenever we think of the elusive "perfect 10.0," most people's minds handspring to the peculiarly compelling world of gymnastics. In an attempt to solve the problem of petty partisanship, the controversial system of scoring has recently been eradicated in favor of an empirical, albeit confusing, new set of rules. Cheryl Hamilton is one of the most respected gymnastics judges in the nation and has helped shepherd in a new era of objectivity and precision. Without getting distracted by the sequins and sparkles, she talks us through what really counts in these gravity-defying competitions.

WOULD YOU PLEASE EXPLAIN THE OLD SYSTEM OF JUDGING VERSUS THE NEW ONE?

Before the mid-2000s when we switched systems, gymnastics judges started with a 10.0 and took all of the execution and compositional deductions from that. Now it's totally different with two sets of judges scoring two different aspects: The difficulty judges are determining whether the gymnast completed a skill—like a simple back-tuck-salto—and then the execution judges say, "Was it high enough, did she have sufficient tuck, and were her toes pointed?" The difficulty judges establish the routine's difficulty value by determining the top eight skills in a gymnast's routine (like a simple leap skill is just an A, but a double-layout with two twists is an I). Then there are some additional factors: When you put certain skills together you get what's called connection value, and there are also five compositional requirements. So when you add everything together, that determines your difficulty value. Then the execution judges evaluate the execution of the routine: things like the bent legs, the bent arms, the insufficient amplitude and so on. They take those deductions from a set 10.0. That score out of 10.0 is then added to the difficulty score, and that's your final score! So if your difficulty start value is a 6.3, and you had a perfect 10.0 execution score, then 16.3 would now technically be your perfect score.

WHY DID THE SYSTEM CHANGE?

Back in the old system, not all perfect 10.0s were created equal. You had gymnasts with easier routines that *just* met the minimum requirements of starting from a 10.0 and then you had gymnasts that far exceeded that difficulty but were also starting from a 10.0. We didn't have the tools to separate them: They were all worth 10.0, but one could be a lot more difficult than the other. Now if a gymnast does a very simple routine in the new system, the routine is worth less. To score highly, you have to do a very good routine with a high difficulty value as well as good execution. It's based on what the gymnast chooses to do and how well she does it.

IF A SO-CALLED "PERFECT SCORE" IS NOW RELATIVE TO THE DIFFICULTY VALUE OF A ROUTINE, WILL THE TOP POSSIBLE PERFECT SCORE CONTINUE TO RISE?

As we continue to progress, gymnasts will do more difficult skills, but the values of the skills will probably change. At the last World Championships, a gymnast did a double-back in stretch position with a double-twist, which we added to our code of points. There are new skills being added all the time so we need to create values for those.

HAS THE CURRENT JUDGING SYSTEM IRONED OUT AS MUCH OF THE SUBJECTIVITY AS IT POSSIBLY CAN?

I think there are still some subjective areas. Artistry on beam and floor is still evaluated by the judges, and they determine whether the gymnast has "personal style." But that's difficult because what's beautiful to me might not be beautiful to somebody else! That's where a lot of subjectivity comes in. That's the human error in the judging system: Everyone's giving their own opinion and everyone's opinion is not the same.

ARE THERE TRENDS IN WHAT CONSTITUTES "PERSONAL STYLE"?

Yes, sometimes we go through a trend where the gymnasts are using classical music and making very elegant routines, and at other times they're using modern music and making more athletic routines. But when we judge, we look at what the gymnast is doing—like classical or athletic—and ask ourselves, "Did she do what she was attempting to do?" Sometimes it's difficult! You have to be very objective and have an open mind. You might not like one type of dance, but you have to say, "I don't like that kind of hip-hop routine. However, she performed that hip-hop routine *great*." And then reward her for that.

DOES THE WORLD OF HAIR, MAKEUP AND STYLING PLAY INTO THE JUDGING PROCESS?

Whenever a gymnast goes out on the floor, we want them to be neat. We don't look at it like a beauty contest, but we certainly wouldn't want them to come out with a lot of clown makeup on or their hair flying around! You obviously want a leotard that's respectful-looking and not real high-cut. But we're not looking at if one girl's leotard is prettier than another. I mean, I hope we're not evaluating that! I don't know whether it plays in our subconscious, but hopefully it doesn't.

WHAT DO VIEWERS NOT REALIZE ABOUT THE RIGOR OF GYMNASTICS JUDGING?

The public doesn't know how strict we have to be. For example, when gymnasts turn on bars they have a degree number they have to turn within, otherwise it's a deduction: If they turn past 45 degrees, it's a higher deduction than if they turn between 30 and 45. It's all very exact.

WHAT HAS JUDGING TAUGHT YOU?

It's taught me to be… I don't know whether the word is "accepting" of things, but I'm a little more open-minded. It's also taught me discipline and focus.

WHAT ELSE HAVE YOU LEARNED THAT YOU CAN APPLY TO EVERYDAY LIFE?

That hard work pays off, not only for the gymnasts and the coaches, but for the judges as well. I've worked hard and I've judged the Olympic Games. Representing my country is just the greatest honor I could ever have. There's some luck in everything, but if you work hard, sometimes you make your luck happen. ○ ○

FEW

ENTERTAINING FOR A FEW

∘ ∘ ∘

PLAYING WITH FIRE: THE BURNED FOOD MENU

Whether you intended it that way or not, some things actually taste better when they're a little crispy around the edges. In this scalding menu, we serve up a meal that encourages the application of a little overzealous heat.

ROASTED BELL PEPPER
BREAD SOUP

CHARRED SPICED LAMB CHOPS
WITH FIGS AND POMEGRANATE

BANANAS FOSTER
FOR DESSERT

RECIPES & FOOD STYLING BY DIANA YEN & THE JEWELS OF NEW YORK
PHOTOGRAPHS BY ALICE GAO & PROP STYLING BY KATE S. JORDAN

ROASTED BELL PEPPER BREAD SOUP

This hearty bell pepper soup is inspired by the classic Italian *pappa al pomodoro*, a type of tomato and bread soup. Our version combines charred bell peppers with day-old bread and nutty almonds for texture. This soup can be enjoyed warm or chilled.

FOR THE SOUP:

6 large red bell peppers,
about 2 1/2 pounds (1.15 kilograms)

4 cups (945 milliliters) chicken or vegetable stock

2 cups (about 70 grams) stale bread,
cut into 1-inch cubes (Italian bread such as
ciabatta or focaccia preferred)

2 garlic cloves, roughly chopped

1/4 cup (55 grams) almonds

Crème fraîche, for garnish

Fresh basil, for garnish

Salt and black pepper, to taste

FOR THE BASIL OIL:

1 cup (30 grams) fresh basil leaves

1/2 cup (120 milliliters) extra-virgin olive oil

Salt, to taste

METHOD Preheat the oven broiler to high. Place the oven rack in the second-highest position. Place the bell peppers on a baking sheet and broil for 15 minutes on each side, until skin is charred and wrinkled. Remove from the oven and let cool. Slice the peppers in half, remove the skin and discard the seeds. (Hint: While still hot, placing the peppers in a sealed plastic bag or in a bowl covered with cling wrap for a few minutes will make the skin easier to remove.) Slice into 1-inch strips and set aside.

Working in batches, place some of the peppers, stock, bread, garlic and almonds in a blender. Puree until smooth. Transfer to a stockpot. Continue with the remaining ingredients. Bring the soup to a boil over medium heat, then reduce to a simmer, and cook for 10 minutes to allow the flavors to develop. Season with salt and pepper to taste.

To make the basil oil, combine the fresh basil, olive oil and salt, and puree until smooth.

Spoon the soup into bowls, top with a dollop of crème fraîche and some torn basil, drizzle lightly with the basil oil and serve.

Serves 6

CHARRED SPICED LAMB CHOPS WITH FIGS AND POMEGRANATE

Searing lamb racks over high heat before placing them in the oven gives results that are charred on the outside and meltingly tender on the inside. This spiced lamb is a perfect combination of sweet and savory, served with figs and pomegranate.

FOR THE SPICE RUB:

2 garlic cloves, minced

2 tablespoons fresh rosemary, finely chopped

1/4 teaspoon ground cumin

1/4 teaspoon turmeric

1/4 teaspoon paprika

1/4 teaspoon ground coriander

1 teaspoon salt

1/2 teaspoon black pepper

1/4 cup (60 milliliters) extra-virgin olive oil

FOR THE LAMB:

2 frenched racks of lamb (8-rib), fat trimmed (each rack about 1 1/2 pounds or 680 grams)

1 tablespoon vegetable oil

6 figs, halved

Cane sugar, for sprinkling

1 tablespoon extra-virgin olive oil

1/2 cup (115 grams) pomegranate seeds, for garnish

Salt and black pepper, to taste

METHOD In a bowl, stir together the garlic, rosemary, spices, salt, pepper and oil. Set aside. Pat the lamb dry and season generously with salt and pepper. Heat a large cast-iron skillet over high heat. Add the vegetable oil to the skillet and brown the lamb racks in two batches, about 2 1/2 minutes per side on both racks. Transfer racks to a roasting pan.

Preheat the oven to 350°F (175°C) with the oven rack in the center. Using a brush, coat the lamb with the spice mixture. Roast for 15–20 minutes until the center of the meat registers 130°F (55°C) when tested with a thermometer. Let stand for 5 minutes.

Meanwhile, sprinkle the sugar over the fig halves. Warm 1 tablespoon of olive oil in a large skillet over medium-high heat. Add the figs to the skillet and cook until softened, turning once, about 2 minutes.

Serve the lamb scattered with the figs and pomegranate seeds.

Serves 6

BANANAS FOSTER

Who can resist the theatrics of a dessert set on fire? This boozy combination of caramelized bananas in rum sauce was invented in New Orleans during the 1950s and has since become a classic on our dining tables. Watch your guests' eyes light up as you ignite this decadent treat. Use caution: Thin glass may crack, so be careful when choosing a vessel.

8 tablespoons (115 grams) unsalted butter

1 1/2 cups (300 grams) dark brown sugar

1 teaspoon ground cinnamon

1/2 teaspoon kosher salt

3 bananas, halved lengthwise, then halved crosswise

3/4 cup (180 milliliters) dark rum

METHOD In a heavy skillet, melt the butter, sugar, cinnamon and salt over medium heat. Cook, stirring often, until the sugar dissolves into the butter. Add the bananas and gently stir until soft, about 3 minutes. Add the rum, and using a match or lighter, ignite the alcohol to flambé! Let the mixture cook until the flame dies out.

To serve, spoon bananas and sauce over scoops of vanilla ice cream or alongside crepes. ○ ○ ○

Serves 6

TURNING OVER A GOLD LEAF

INTERVIEW BY TAE INO & PHOTOGRAPHS BY HIDEAKI HAMADA

The ancient Japanese art form of kintsugi uses gold leaf to repair cracked ceramics, emphasizing the pottery's damaged history rather than hiding it. We spoke with Tokyo-based repairer Michihiro Hori about the tradition.

CAN YOU PLEASE TELL US ABOUT THE HISTORY OF *KINTSUGI* IN JAPAN?

It started in the Muromachi period when the tea ceremony culture—known as *chanoyu* or *sado*—became popular. Instead of concealing the damage done to these ceramics, kintsugi makes beautiful art out of the repair process and appreciates the new life given to the repaired item. I've been doing kintsugi for about six years, but before that I did all types of lacquer work for almost 20 years.

HOW DOES THE ART OF KINTSUGI RELATE TO JAPAN'S LIFESTYLE AND CULTURE?

It has a lot to do with the Japanese philosophy of *wabi-sabi,* which is about cherishing and taking good care of things while also embracing their flaws, especially as they age and come closer to their natural form. The art of kintsugi is in the beauty of its transformation. It gives items a new life, a fresh start.

PLEASE DESCRIBE THE PROCESS OF REPAIRING A PIECE.

After you've cleaned, sanded and prepared the broken pieces, you make a mix of water, flour and *kiurushi*—a type of raw lacquer—and put the pieces back together using a bamboo spatula. Once completed, you put it in a drying box called a *muro* for two weeks. Next, you shave off the excess lacquer, smooth it with sandpaper and then begin the decorating process: This involves many different materials such as *roiro-urushi, e-urushi* and finally the gold powder. You let it all dry before doing a final layer of kiurushi and oil, polishing the seams until they shine.

APART FROM GOLD LEAF, WHAT OTHER MATERIALS CAN YOU USE?

Gold has always been the finest metal material, and it's also considered the prestigious choice to highlight and illuminate repairs. However, you can also use silver, tin and brass.

WHO ARE YOUR REGULAR CLIENTS?

I take orders from antique shops and also directly from customers. It takes a few weeks to do a repair, but right now I have so many back orders that I'm booked up for six months to a year. I'm so busy with my main job as a cartoonist and illustrator that it's becoming hard to make time to do repairs!

HOW POPULAR IS KINTSUGI IN MODERN JAPAN?

When we were materially poor, it was natural for people to repair and use something for as long as they could. And recently, especially after the earthquake in 2011, more people seem to be taking an interest in kintsugi. Repair orders have increased, as well as the number of people who want to learn the craft.

WHAT'S YOUR FAVORITE PART ABOUT KINTSUGI REPAIR?

I've had a lot of setbacks and discouragement in my life, so I appreciate kintsugi's simple lesson—that it's possible to start over. ○ ○ ○

Tae Ino is a writer and editor who lives in Tokyo. She also designs, knits and sells original items, and enjoys dancing, picnicking, cooking and taking naps.

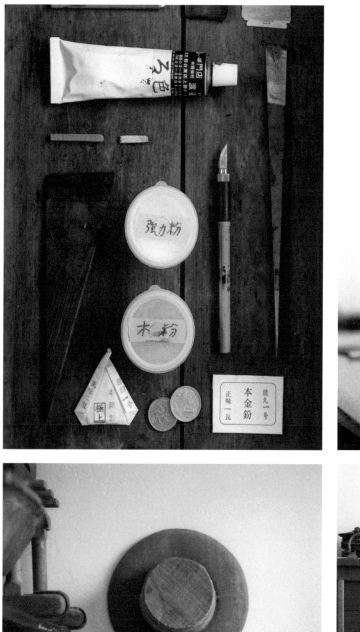

IN WITH THE OLD

Some folks buy a history-filled home and demolish it entirely, choosing to fill the clean slate with sharp lines and modern designs. Others revel in the stories a house can hold, appreciating its architectural quirks that keep the original soul alive. We visit two homes in Europe that bask in this patched-up aesthetic.

WORDS BY SARAH ROWLAND & PHOTOGRAPHS BY WICHMANN + BENDTSEN

STYLING & PRODUCTION BY HELLE WALSTED

THE ANCIENT BLACKSMITHERY *Lesbos, Greece*

"Imperfection is part of life: It's where the poetry and humor hide," says Dorte Mandrup-Poulsen, an architect living in Denmark. In keeping with this ethos, she and two other Danish architects (Louis Becker and Jens Thomas Arnfred) have made an old blacksmith's warehouse their shared second home on the Greek island of Lesbos. Spending their summers by the sea, the designers and their families have vacationed together for years. "We all lived in Denmark but liked to go on vacation with all the families in the summer," she says. "We've owned it for eight years now, and the kids have a long history together." Made up of small coastal towns and villages, Lesbos is located in the northeastern corner of the Aegean Sea and is known for its enchanting landscapes. The small village of Plomari sits south of Mount Olympus and is unaffected by tourism, preserving a sense of Greek Old World tradition. "We liked the town for being very authentic," she says. Houses of

all different shapes, sizes and colors make up the eclectic architecture of the city as well as semi-rundown factories, abandoned buildings and old mansions that are backdropped by lush forests of olive trees and fronted by bright blue seascapes. In the middle of it all sits a former blacksmith: The 1930s building had been abandoned for a while before Dorte and her architecture fellows redesigned and renovated the space in 2009. The original stone construction consisted of a single open room, so they built a wooden structure in one end of the space (containing beds, a kitchen area and a bathroom) to create more nooks. Staying true to the original character of the warehouse and working to preserve its older features, the architects appreciated the home for its weathered and lived-in feel. "It's important when you convert an old building to be careful not to remove the soul of what was there. If everything is renewed, it becomes too perfect," Dorte says.

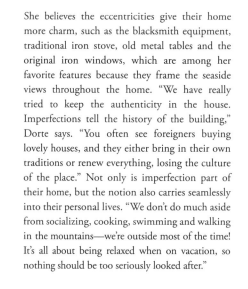

She believes the eccentricities give their home more charm, such as the blacksmith equipment, traditional iron stove, old metal tables and the original iron windows, which are among her favorite features because they frame the seaside views throughout the home. "We have really tried to keep the authenticity in the house. Imperfections tell the history of the building," Dorte says. "You often see foreigners buying lovely houses, and they either bring in their own traditions or renew everything, losing the culture of the place." Not only is imperfection part of their home, but the notion also carries seamlessly into their personal lives. "We don't do much aside from socializing, cooking, swimming and walking in the mountains—we're outside most of the time! It's all about being relaxed when on vacation, so nothing should be too seriously looked after."

THE FORMER PASTRY FACTORY *Paris, France*

When industrial designer Stéphane Quatresous first discovered a hidden Parisian manufacturer's warehouse once used as a pastry-cutting factory, he knew he wanted to make it his home. Tucked away in a remote alleyway in the vibrant 11th arrondissement, the building had a secluded feel that made it feel like a much-needed escape from the city. "The road is impassable by car," he says. "It's made of old cobblestones and remains in the original condition. It's also surrounded by wild grasses, herbs, flowers and gardens, which is unusual for Paris." The weathered feel of the exterior offers a warm welcome that Stéphane has consciously tried to preserve while decorating the home's interior. Using natural light, shades of earth tones and artistic touches, he was able to complement the features on the inside while staying true to the factory feel of the building. "The outside is the first impression, then you enter and can feel the unique design and the actual spirit of the place," he says. In maintaining the original aesthetic, pieces of the building have remained dilapidated: Stéphane kept the traditional patina of the factory walls, the old windows and exposed wooden beams to embrace the charm and soul. "It's very cozy and so different from most spaces in Paris," he says. "It feels like home—you feel well." In 2007, he started designing his own furniture and later opened Atelier 154, a showroom showcasing items that become better with age, featuring brushed metal, oxidized steel and raw wood. "Each material wears in a very different way, and imperfections are unique to each object. You'll never find the same scratch twice," he says. Instead of covering up the irregularities, his designs and decorating techniques highlight wear and tear. Mirroring the aesthetic of his renovated factory house, the showroom is a true extension of his home: Electrical insulators have been repurposed as stools, old lightbulbs are displayed in vases, and discs from circular saws line the floors. Taking old materials and merging them with something new, he aims to create products that don't feel manufactured. "The designs are not perfect, but they are made that way on purpose," he says. From his work as a furniture designer to his life in the Parisian factory building, Stéphane doesn't consider perfection to be the ideal dream. "There is an act of refusing logic when creating and designing," he says. "It's inspiring to find the transformation and unity to bring it all together in the end." ○ ○ ○

TWO OF A KIND

WORDS BY JOHN STANLEY & ILLUSTRATION BY SARAH JACOBY

It's difficult to curate a sock collection when one of each pair always manages to lose itself in the laundry room, but there are ways to keep your mind in order even when your sock drawer isn't.

There are three certainties in life: death, taxes and losing socks. Throughout your life, every one of the pairs you buy will consciously uncouple. The hows and whys of the losses are ultimately irrelevant but must be reluctantly accepted, like war and Justin Bieber. Whether you choose to wear supermarket multipacks, Peruvian vicuña yarn or nålebinded designs you just spun yourself, all pairs of socks are just like marriages: frequently ending in divorce, with a partner left behind and forcibly assigned to cleaning duties. So when adulthood finally called and the responsibility became my own, I attempted to solve the problem once and for all—by making my sock collection entirely black. No pairing, no need to scrabble in a drawer, no ugly break-ups.

I probably thought I was the first person to feel real love as well. But I noticed that my collection of black socks of different styles, brands and ages gradually dissolved into entropy and chaos, like a sergeant-less platoon: The blacks became navy-of-the-night or dungeon-gray at will. Being at least part-geek, I generally prefer order and organization, and wearing nearly-but-not-quite mismatched socks drove me crazy. Pairing my body of black socks gradually became more and more difficult as I had to start looking closely for length, stitching and shade. The time burden was ridiculous. Eventually I threw the lot out and bought an entirely new, identical black set from one shop, a strategy so staggeringly wasteful and indulgent that I've felt guilty about it ever since. This new underwear Holocene didn't last forever either: They still all wore out at different rates, and my sense of order raged.

The Japanese have a concept called *wabi-sabi* that values impermanence, flaws and processes that seem natural. The knobbly hand-thrown pot, the autumn leaves scattered on the grass, the running sock stuck between the inner and outer drum—all are part of the flux of existence, all to be contemplated and accepted. *Why are you trying to force order upon something that actively resists it? You can't win, you know.* Or can you?

I asked around. A decidedly more neurotic friend of mine buys 10 black pairs at a time and sews a small loop of colored cotton into each one. The next year, 10 more black pairs and a different color loop; this way he can keep track of different series. Another friend employs the all-black strategy, culling annually between Christmas and the New Year and replenishing from the same shop—though this leaves him vulnerable to well-meaning relatives buying the wrong kind of socks as presents. Yet another mate invariably throws away all her socks every time she moves and buys a whole new set—the springtime sentiment is wonderful, but the profligacy problematic. Sock protocols, like betting systems to beat the casinos, always have some lurking flaw.

So finally, I have relaxed. I buy colors, stripes, whatever. I operate a simple but strict herding system where those without a partner languish on "Sock Row" on top of the dresser until they are reunited— *or worse*. It's harsh, but just. I've finally accepted that socks are a traveling band of messy, frustrating, constantly changing members. When I want to see a blissful reminder of the transience of all things, I just look in my sock drawer. ○ ○ ○

John Stanley is a writer and musician living and working in London. He writes about archery at theinfinitecurve.com and worldarchery.org.

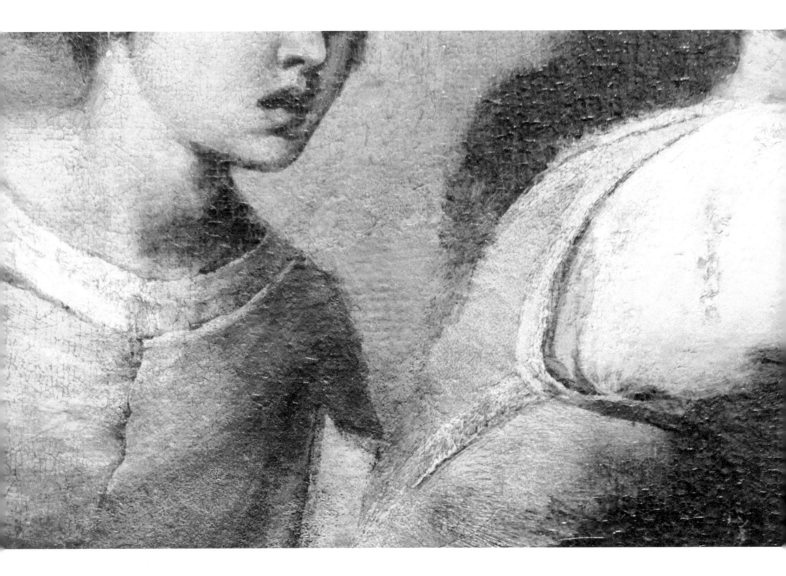

TO CONSERVE AND PROTECT

Many pieces of fine art have suffered through a lot, from being lost in a humid attic for centuries to canvases slashed in jealous fits of rage. It's an art conservator's job to decide what damage to restore and what revealing faults to preserve.

WORDS BY JOANNA HAN &
PHOTOGRAPHS BY SHANTANU STARICK

Muirne Lydon is a paintings conservator at the National Gallery of Ireland, working as part of a team that oversees the care for more than 15,000 paintings, sculptures, works on paper and objets d'art to the highest possible standards. Balancing an artistic sensibility with scientific and technical knowledge, the painter-turned-conservator deals primarily with imperfections in art caused by the effects of age, whether it's the natural degradation of centuries-old paint or the damage from years of improper storage. "It's a role that equals part art historian, artist, scientist and sleuth," she explains. "A few decades ago, much restoration work was done by people guessing the original materials, but today's conservators are more likely to have a grounding in chemistry and physics."

A gem of the gallery's wide-ranging collection is a series of six paintings by the Spanish Baroque painter Bartolomé Esteban Murillo (1617–1682). Muirne is the lead conservator on the grand project to conserve these works and uncover new insight into Murillo's technique. Using strong light, dark shadows, rich emotion and vivid colors, the series dramatically depicts the parable of the Prodigal Son in typical Baroque style. For centuries the paintings were moved, traded, purchased and passed down between the hands of queens, popes and earls, and eventually donated to the National Gallery of Ireland in 1987. They were in poor condition when they arrived: "The clarity of the paintings was greatly reduced because of their severely degraded varnish layers,"

Muirne says. "They appeared very yellowed, and Murillo's delicate range of light-to-dark modeling was greatly distorted."

Several of the pieces had also suffered an unfortunate overzealous cleaning in the 1960s, leaving them deteriorated with abrasion and crude varnish work. Conservators often deal with correcting badly done past restorations as well as the degradation of materials. "I frequently feel like an archaeologist working at a micro-level, painstakingly removing years of dirt and old restorations to reveal Murillo's beautiful brushwork and light handling of paint," she says.

Through using thorough technical analysis including x-rays, infrared photography, material sampling and other forms of examination, conservators can gain a clear understanding of the artist's working methods. An out-of-place, heavy brushstroke or a seemingly discolored section might be revealed to be a mark of the artist's hand, not an accidental addition from history. "This is one of the sides of conservation that I really love—the idea that you can step back in time and see exactly how an artist created a masterpiece," Muirne says. "Conservators are in the fortunate position to not only see the final painting but the entire process an artist has gone through to arrive at a finished piece. With scientific analysis, I feel as if I'm sitting beside the artists as they're creating their masterpieces."

The ultimate objective of the conservator is not to achieve technical perfection, but rather to ensure that the artist's original intention is honored and communicated. More often than not, old works simply can't be restored to their original condition, so the mitigation of imperfections is the next best thing. "My number one priority is the care of the collection," she says. "I feel like I'm part of an ongoing story of history, and I'm just looking after the works for this part of their journey." ○ ○ ○

Joanna Han is a contributing editor at Kinfolk. *She lives, writes and drinks good coffee in Portland, Oregon, but is scheming to move to Sweden.*

DREAM WEAVERS

WORDS BY NICOLE VARVITSIOTES & PHOTOGRAPH BY CRAIG JOHNSON

Drawing from Navajo legend, the native weavers of Spider Rock have been incorporating purposeful imperfections into their designs for years. Intended as a way to keep their minds unattached and open to progress, this humble practice can teach us a lot about our own creative processes.

High above the sun-punished floor of Canyon de Chelly in a sandstone spire known as Spider Rock, Spider Woman once wove on a loom that Spider Man made for her out of sunshine, lightning and rain. While the details of this Navajo folklore have become elusive with time, native weaver Emily Malone—whose family has created distinct Spider Rock designs for generations—explains how her people learned to weave:

"It's only in winter that we tell the story about twin boys who made a journey to their father, the sun," Emily says. "On the way they met Spider Woman, and she invited them into her house. It was a small home, and the boys asked her how they could fit in. Suddenly, a big opening appeared for them to go through, and inside were all different kinds of weavings. She told them to let their mother come and she would teach her how to weave."

Through studying Spider Woman's craft, the Navajo people learned to make blankets that brought warmth during harsh winters and offered new opportunities for trade. As a tribute to her, many weavers deliberately left a hole in the center of their blankets—one that mirrored the hole in the center of a spider web, and possibly the hole through which the twins entered Spider Woman's home.

But over time, buyers started to see these holes as design flaws: imperfections on products that were otherwise perfect. Closing them would have meant opening the weavers up to potentially adverse spiritual consequences, so as a compromise, some weavers began to include what are now called "spirit lines" into their work instead. A non-structural variation of imperfection, spirit lines are created by using a contrasting thread in the same color as the background to add intentional breaks in a weaving's geometric borders. Where they're placed, their length and how many rows they claim are all matters of the weaver's personal taste; the only common thread is the significance drawn from their intent.

While spirit lines may still be perceived as purposeful mistakes to some, Emily describes them as beautiful. In her culture, they're referred to as *shih nih bi-teen*, which translates to "my mind's road." Her family believes that spirit lines are intentionally placed pathways meant to release their minds from their handiwork, preventing their creativity from being trapped in the weaving forever. "Spirit lines are important to us," she says. "They keep your mind open for your next project. Without them, you enclose your designs in one rug and won't be able to think of the next one."

Spirit lines are a means of releasing energy, a doorway to the future, a pathway that connects a weaver's first rug to her last using creative momentum to propel her designs forward. Without that contrasting line, the weaver's design may appear aesthetically perfect, but reaching perfection has its consequences: If it's attained, there's nowhere left to go, no work left to be done.

If a spirit line is a visual reminder to push creative boundaries, then it's a symbol that can extend beyond the Navajo nation. It can live in paintings or pastries, songs or sculptures. How it takes shape is at the will of the artist, but to those who make art or food or photographs, incorporating tangible evidence of a beautifully imperfect journey offers the mind a road to betterment. ○ ○ ○

Nicole Varvitsiotes is a writer always on the lookout for silver linings. A contributor to The Daily Muse, Forbes *and* Mashable, *she lives in San Luis Obispo, California.*

CULINARY CALAMITIES

Even the best of us screw up sometimes.
Six chefs from Portland, Oregon, tell us about their
tales of injury, survival and epic fails.

JASON FRENCH: chef/owner, Ned Ludd
INGRID CHEN: chef, Remedy Wine Bar
JOHANNA WARE: chef/owner, Smallwares
JOHN GORHAM: chef/owner, Toro Bravo and Tasty n Sons
SCOTT DOLICH: chef/owner, Park Kitchen and the Bent Brick
GABRIEL RUCKER: chef/owner, Le Pigeon and Little Bird Bistro

PHOTOGRAPH BY ANJA VERDUGO & STYLING BY ALISON BRISLIN

WHAT DISHES HAVE YOU COME UP WITH AFTER SCREWING UP SOMETHING ELSE?

Jason: Over-cured lamb loin has become a signature piece for hors d'oeuvres and starters on our recent tasting menus. It started when we essentially left some lamb in an olive brine and then forgot about it for about four days. The result was a sublime piece of meat we serve thinly sliced with fermented kale, smoked butter and black olive crumbs.

Ingrid: Brown butter hollandaise was born one Thanksgiving three years ago during an intense two-day cooking extravaganza that was part of meeting my now-husband's family for the first time. It was the final half hour before dinner: The turkey was resting, the bread and stuffing were being pulled from the oven and sauces were getting finished. We were serving a hollandaise with roasted delicata squash, and in an effort to make clarified butter, I overzealously clarified it and accidentally browned the milk solids. After a moment of panic, it struck me that brown butter hollandaise wouldn't be the worst thing in the world, so I continued the classic hollandaise method with my nutty clarified butter and mixed in some of the browned solids to amp up the flavor. The sweet-savory-salty taste of the squash and browned butter turned into one of the winners of the dinner.

Johanna: When I first opened Smallwares, it was winter and there wasn't a lot of produce available. I was frying butternut squash and tossing it with fish sauce, bacon and mint. It had so much potential, but it was too meaty for what I was trying to achieve. I was searching for any substitution, so when kale came back in season, I dipped a leaf in tempura batter and fried it: It was so light, crispy and delicious. It has now become our signature dish.

Scott: My most famous happy accident was the chickpea fries at Park Kitchen. I created them while experimenting with *socca*, the delicious chickpea pancakes served in southern France.

The batter I made was too thick so I ended up trying to cook it like polenta. It was a sticky, gluey mess. I poured it out on a sheet, stuck it in the walk-in fridge and forgot about it. At the end of the night, I cut it into strips and deep-fried it for a staff meal. Everyone loved them.

Gabriel: I was making a lobster cream sauce—essentially lobster stock made with heavy cream—and I let it boil away for too long. The result was a separated and extremely flavorful concoction, or two to be exact: one a lobster stock, the other a lobster butter of sorts.

John: A line cook once over-roasted some hazelnuts that were meant to go into a salad, but that wasn't going to happen anymore! Instead of throwing them out, we turned them into a dark roasted hazelnut ice cream base.

WHAT SCARS, INJURIES OR WAR WOUNDS HAVE YOU SUFFERED IN THE KITCHEN?

John: This is more a close call than a war wound, but in '93 I was working at the Mural Room in Wyoming as a saucier, and during a staff meal everyone had left the kitchen except a dishwasher and myself. We were standing about 10 feet away from each other. Somebody had left a can of pan spray on the flattop. It got so hot that it exploded and pieces of metal shrapnel went shooting through the kitchen. The biggest piece must have been going a hundred miles an hour. It went through two walls and got lodged into a third. If it had hit me, it would have taken my head off.

Johanna: When I was at Public in New York, I pulled a pan of braising oxtail out of the oven and my hand slipped. Hot jus poured into one of my clogs and I could feel the skin peel off. I acted as if nothing had happened, threw the oxtail on the table and went into the office. I ripped my sock off and there was a two-inch square of skin missing. I slathered burn cream on it, wrapped it in gauze, put my sock back on and finished my shift. I had

burned all the nerve endings off the top of my foot and my non–health insurance clinic in Queens brought the whole staff into the room to look at how burned my foot was. The worst part was that we were so understaffed I worked through it: I would just sit on a crate and do prep!

Jason: So many! Mini cuts and nicks happen all the time. Hopefully you aren't working the salad station where vinegar and lemon juice can make for a long night! The worst was when I spilled a 10-gallon stockpot of fryer oil on my foot, leaving second- and third-degree burns on my lower leg and the top of my foot. If something happens during work, you use line triage and just keep cooking: Mustard is great for big burns since it's anti-microbial/bacterial, and Super Glue works well for big cuts that won't stop bleeding.

Ingrid: I've gotten them all—burns, cuts, punctures, blisters and sundry scars—but the worst injury was while searing about 40 lamb shanks in the middle of service for an overnight braise. Tickets were coming in and with one very quick turn of a shank, I splashed searing hot lamb fat against the side of the pan and onto my face. The skin blistered off immediately and I had two second-degree burns on my cheek and chin, each about the size of a quarter. I was in terrible pain... and continued cooking for the remainder of service.

Scott: The worst scars I have are from the tandoori oven at Wildwood in Portland, Oregon, which is now closed. We cooked naan to order on the sides of the ceramic oven: We'd stretch out the dough and slap it onto the sides of the oven through a small opening on top. I'd often hit my forearm on the 900°F ceramic lip of the oven, leaving a ring of burn welts on my arm. I now have a permanent scar ringed around my forearm—it's kind of cool, but it sucked enduring the pain on a continual basis. I thought the scars would never heal.

WHAT'S THE MOST EMBARRASSING THING YOU'VE SEEN HAPPEN BEHIND THE SCENES IN A KITCHEN THAT THE PATRONS WERE BLISSFULLY UNAWARE OF?

Jason: I worked at one restaurant where the power went out in the kitchen for hours. There were no lights, so we cooked with mini flashlights in our mouths for an hour until they came back on. Hysterical.

John: It's always funny to see a new cook use a powerful commercial blender without a lid on and watch them dress themselves with whatever it is they're blending. It doesn't happen often though—once had better be enough to learn your lesson!

Johanna: After struggling with sales for so long at Smallwares, we were having one of our best Friday nights and we were packed. All of a sudden I could smell the grease trap—I turned around and it was overflowing. We have an open kitchen and the smell was so awful that I started to panic. We had to unclog it, clean it up and run service. It was one of the craziest nights of my career. I still get short of breath when I think about it.

WOULD YOU PLEASE TELL US ABOUT THE BIGGEST COOKING DISASTER YOU'VE HAD IN A COMMERCIAL KITCHEN? HOW DID YOU RECOVER FROM IT?

Scott: I once had a whole pig that I was spit-roasting on the patio of the Bent Brick in Portland, Oregon, catch on fire in front of all my customers. There was no fix for this one: It was toast. The only redeeming factor was that no one was hurt and there was some entertainment value for my patio customers.

Jason: At Fore Street in Portland, Maine, I once sent a whole pork loin flying across the line out on to the floor of the dining room. I froze, and [James Beard Award–winning chef] Sam Hayward muttered without moving his lips, "Go pick that up... *now*." It's a classic tale.

Gabriel: We have an open kitchen, so our patrons are aware of *everything*. We once spilled grease on the flattop, which caught the kitchen on fire and there was no hiding it. Luckily we got it taken care of and the show went on. We still have the smoke marks on the copper.

John: Once we had a fire in the fryer from carbon buildup. Luckily the sprinkler system didn't go off, but we had to use the fire extinguisher, which gets nasty powder on everything. Typically you'd have to close for a few days, but our crew rallied. We threw out all the food on the line, reprinted a limited menu with what we could prep in a few hours and deep-cleaned the restaurant from top to bottom: Every plate, glass, utensil, pot, pan, *everything* went through the dishwasher. The walls, the floor... I mean *every* inch of the restaurant got scrubbed. I had a new fryer delivered within an hour. We got permission from the health department to reopen, salvaged the flowers from the broken vase that the firemen knocked over and opened an hour later than normal. I've never seen our staff so united.

WHAT LESSONS HAVE YOU LEARNED AT HOME?

Jason: Salad dressing can't be used as pasta sauce.

Scott: The most notorious disaster I've executed at home was trying to spit-cook a goat for my family. It was an all-day affair at a family reunion. It ended up being tough as nails—literally inedible. My parents made T-shirts for the whole family mocking my screwup saying "Eat less goat."

John: I was given a Crock-Pot for Christmas and tried to re-create my mom's Crock-Pot chicken, which I remember being so good. It turned out bland, mushy and inedible.

DO YOU FOLLOW RECIPES METHODICALLY AND MEASURE INGREDIENTS CORRECTLY, OR JUST THROW IN WHATEVER SUITS IN THE MOMENT?

Johanna: I'm horrible with measuring! I work on instinct and flavor. I just throw ingredients together and can't even remember what I did the next day. After two years of owning a restaurant, I've finally started to measure and document things: It's a huge step. But I still spontaneously tweak a dish during service and forget to tell my sous chefs!

Jason: Classic techniques are there for a reason, and ratios are the foundation of those. Understanding ingredients goes a long way, but we "cook from the hip" while rooted in tradition. We don't use recipes since they're merely guides, not laws.

WHAT HAVE YOU LEARNED ABOUT PERFECTION? CAN A DISH EVER BE PERFECT?

Ingrid: I believe a meal can be perfect for a diner, but as a cook, there will always be something you could do better. There are a million tiny decisions that have to be made in the course of a day (when to turn the steak, where to put your knife in the side of a fish, how much salt you add to the potatoes) and not every one will be perfect.

Jason: I use a wood-fired oven to cook almost everything, so I've gotten used to having things come out imperfectly. I really try to stay away from the idea of perfection in most things and find true beauty in life's imperfection. Nature tells us time and time again that the world is process.

John: It takes a lot of screwing up to learn.

Johanna: I've definitely always felt a bit barbaric in the kitchen and that I lack finesse. I sometimes equate beautiful plating and precision with perfection and know I can't achieve that. I've come to terms with knowing my own limitations and working around them. The minute you think you've achieved perfection, you stop learning.

Gabriel: Well, we have a saying: "Make it a jewel." Sometimes the imperfect is perfect. Someone's cooking can be perfect for one person at a specific time, but you're bound to disappoint someone on any given night. The goal is to make that happen as little as possible. ○ ○ ○

A LETTER FROM LEFTY

WORDS BY GEORGIA FRANCES KING & PHOTOGRAPH BY ANJA VERDUGO

Dear Mr. Right,

My sincerest apologies in advance if you struggle to read this note, if not for its radical honesty then for the fact that my fountain pen's ink is smudging across the paper.

As the Thelma to your Louise, I'd like to tell you a little about life on my side of the vertical equator. After all, there are upsides to being a southpaw.

While only one in ten humans is a lefty, there's a lopsided contingent that has made history. For every left-handed psychopath such as Jack the Ripper or Alexander the Great, there has been a genius counterpart in Einstein or Leonardo da Vinci. Since the end of WWII, more than half of the US presidents have been left-handed—including Obama and Clinton—and there are a disproportionate number of us among Mensa's ranks. We may be potential sorcerers to the Inuit and cursed to Moroccans, but we're also healers to the Incas and luck-filled to the Zuni.

It's no surprise that my moniker's etymology isn't in my favor either. Why do women never seek Mr. Left? Why does a leader have his right-hand man but the uncoordinated have two left feet? And it expands beyond the Queen's English: The Italians share one word for both *sinister* and *left*, as well as *treacherous* and *left-handed*, and the word for *clumsy* in German refers to us too. Even the term *ambidextrous* comes from the Latin "to be right on both sides." I'll never win.

Everything in this world that was built for your palms is a challenge we must surmount. Scissors that don't cut. Can openers that don't open. Computer mice that don't click. Power tools that risk accidental catastrophic hemorrhages. We knock elbows when eating at tables and poke eyes with bows when playing in orchestras. Even the humble handshake is in your favor.

However, there are aspects of life where we do have an advantage. The left side of the body is controlled by the right side of the brain, but we use the left's neurons more on a day-to-day basis. Because of this daily communication, it means we form stronger neural pathways between the hemispheres, making us quicker decision makers, faster processers and better multitaskers. And it goes beyond the cranial too: With 3,400 words to be typed solely using the left hand versus 450 words with the right, we're faster typists. We don't have to swap our forks to our eating hand when cutting up and consuming dinner. With our proclivity to choose the left line over the right, we spend less time standing in lines by default (even Disneyland officials say so). We adapt to seeing underwater more clearly. We're less likely to get arthritis or ulcers.

But quirkiness aside, shall I tell you what's ultimately in our favor? Evolution.

If we really were at such a disadvantage, Darwin's theory of natural selection would have cast us off eons ago. But here we still are. And why? Combat. That's correct—if it came down to you and me in a fistfight, evolution has determined that I'll always have the slightest advantage. When you were growing up as a Neanderthal more than 400,000 years ago, you became more acquainted with dueling with right-handers. So when a lefty suddenly jumped out of a cave and confronted your tribe, each jab we threw came at a surprising angle and gave us the proverbial upper hand. It's what makes us better baseball batters and Olympic fencers, and it's the reason nature has deemed us worthy of biological selection. In the long term, it is I who will reign.

So what do you say, Mr. Right? Can we shake on this? ○ ○ ○

Regards,

Lefty

BLOOD ORANGE AND BOURBON MARMALADE

RECIPE BY SUZANNE FUOCO

B oozy jam for breakfast? Why not? Suzanne Fuoco of Pink Slip Jam gives us an easy-peasy recipe for a slightly salacious preserve to either jump-start our day or end it on a sweet note.

INGREDIENTS	TOOLS
8 medium blood oranges	Large stainless-steel or enamel saucepan
4 lemons (Meyer lemons preferred)	8 (8-ounce) canning jars
4 cups (1 liter) water	Canning pot with lid and rack
1 cup (235 milliliters) bourbon	Jar lifter
5 cups (1 kilogram) granulated sugar	Ladle
1 teaspoon ground cloves	Widemouthed canning funnel

METHOD Squeeze the juice from the oranges, discarding the white pith and seeds. Remove the rind of the oranges with a vegetable peeler or a zester, slicing the rind into thin strips. Put the rind, orange juice and pulp into a large saucepan.

Repeat the process with the lemons by squeezing the juice out, discarding the white pith and seeds, and then removing the rind and slicing it into thin strips. Add the lemon juice, rind, water and bourbon to the saucepan containing the orange ingredients. Bring to a boil over high heat, then reduce heat. Cover and boil gently for 30 minutes.

Meanwhile, place the jars on a canning rack and submerge completely in water. Bring the water to a simmer while you finish the marmalade. Place the lid centers in a small saucepan. Cover with water and bring to a simmer.

Add the sugar and cloves to the saucepan of citrus and bring back to a rapid boil. Continue to boil rapidly uncovered while stirring frequently, about 15 to 30 minutes, or until the mixture forms a gel. Test for the right gel stage by drizzling small amount of marmalade on a plate that has been chilled in the freezer, then turning the plate at an angle. If the tiny bit of jam runs down quickly, it needs further cooking. If it slowly moves down the plate or stops, it is done. Remove the marmalade from the heat.

Remove the jars carefully from the hot water and ladle the marmalade into them using the widemouthed funnel, leaving 1/4-inch at the top for any expansion. Drain and apply the jam lid and rings, and twist on loosely until secure, but don't tighten.

Place the jars of jam on the rack of the canner containing hot water. Adjust the water level to cover the jars by approximately 1 inch. Cover the canner and bring the water to a boil.

Process the jars for 10 minutes: Start counting the processing time once the water has come to a steady boil. When the processing time is over, turn off the heat and remove the lid from the canner. Allow the jars to remain in the water for 5 minutes to stabilize the pressure inside them. After 5 minutes, use a jar lifter or lift the rack from the water by the handles. Do not place jars on a cold surface or they may crack. Place them on towels or a wooden cutting board and allow 24 hours to cool.

Unopened jams and marmalades will be preserved for 1 year. Refrigerate after opening. ○ ○ ○

Makes eight 8-ounce jars

Suzanne Fuoco runs Pink Slip Jam, a small-batch business making jams, marmalades and chutneys using organic, seasonal and mostly local fruits. She makes her jams fresh in Portland, Oregon.